Social Work Practice with Adults

Edited by
DIANE GALPIN AND
NATALIE BATES

Series Editor: Keith Brown

LearningMatters

First published in 2009 by Learning Matters Ltd
Reprinted in 2010

British Library Cataloguing in Publication Data
A CIP record for this book is available from the British Library.

ISBN: 978 1 84445 292 7

Cover and text design by Code 5 Design Associates Ltd
Project management by Swales & Willis
Typeset by Swales & Willis Ltd, Exeter, Devon
Printed and bound in Great Britain by TJ International, Padstow, Cornwall

Learning Matters Ltd
33 Southernhay East
Exeter EX1 1NX
Tel: 01392 215560
info@learningmatters.co.uk
www.learningmatters.co.uk

FSC
Mixed Sources
Product group from well-managed
forests and other controlled sources
Cert no. SGS-COC-2482
www.fsc.org
© 1996 Forest Stewardship Council

Social Work Practice with Adults

Post-Qualifying Social Work Practice – other titles in this series

The Approved Mental Health Professional's Guide to Mental
  Health Law (second edition)   ISBN 978 1 84445 115 9
The Approved Mental Health Professional's Guide to Psychiatry
  and Medication (second edition)   ISBN 978 1 84445 304 7
Critical Thinking for Social Work (second edition)   ISBN 978 1 84445 157 9
Evidence-based Policy and Practice in Mental Health
  Social Work   ISBN 978 1 84445 149 4
The Integration of Mental Health Social Work and the NHS   ISBN 978 1 84445 150 0
Introducing Child Care Social Work: Contemporary Policy
  and Practice   ISBN 978 1 84445 180 7
Law and the Social Work Practitioner (second edition)   ISBN 978 1 84445 264 4
Leadership, Management and Supervision in Health and
  Social Care   ISBN 978 1 84445 181 4
Managing with Plans and Budgets in Health and Social Care   ISBN 978 1 84445 134 0
The Mental Capacity Act 2005: A Guide for Practice
  (second edition)   ISBN 978 1 84445 294 1
Newly Qualified Social Workers: A Handbook for Practice   ISBN 978 1 84445 251 4
Practice Education in Social Work   ISBN 978 1 84445 105 0
Practising Quality Assurance in Social Care   ISBN 978 1 84445 084 8
Proactive Management in Social Work Practice   ISBN 978 1 84445 289 7
Social Work Practice with Older Lesbians and Gay Men   ISBN 978 1 84445 182 1
Vulnerable Adults and Community Care (second edition)   ISBN 978 1 84445 362 7

To order, please contact our distributor: BEBC Distribution, Albion Close, Parkstone, Poole, BH12 3LL. Telephone: 0845 230 9000, email: **learningmatters@bebc.co.uk.**

You can also find more information on each of these titles and our other learning resources at **www.learningmatters.co.uk**

Contents

Foreword to the Post-Qualifying Social Work
   Practice Series   vii

About the authors   viii

Acknowledgements   ix

Introduction   x

1 Personalisation: from consumer rights to human rights   1

Diane Galpin

2 Working with older people: managing risk and promoting interdependence   16

Emma Perry

3 The rising profile of informal care: modernisation and the future of carers' services   33

Sally Lee

4 Assessment and practice in learning disability services   49

Jill Small

5 Direct payments and older people: developing a framework for practice   70

Elizabeth Burrow

6   **Transformation: a future for social work
     practice?**   **88**

Diane Galpin

References   107
Index   120

Foreword to the Post-Qualifying Social Work Practice Series

This new text, which has been edited by Diane Galpin and Natalie Bates, is the result of a significant collaboration between social work practitioners and students on one of the many Bournemouth University Post-Qualifying Social Work programmes.

This book successfully captures the reflections and experiences of practitioners in adult social work practice and considers a host of contemporary issues including the impact of personalisation, direct payments, and the transformation agenda. Practical activities have been included in each chapter which are designed to encourage critical debate and which will allow readers to reflect upon their personal practice experiences.

I'd like to thank all contributors for their input and I'd also like to thank the editors for their dedication and insight. The result is an up-to-date text which explores many of the current issues surrounding social work practice with adults and which will be a most useful resource for students. Adult social work practice is a rapidly changing environment, especially with the current 'transformation' agenda in adult social care, and so this text is of particular relevance to all practitioners working in this field.

Whether you are a student on, or about to commence, a Post-Qualifying Social Work Award programme, or whether you are an experienced practitioner in this field, I am sure that this text and its insightful analysis will prove to be invaluable.

Keith Brown
Director of the Centre for Post-Qualifying Social Work
Bournemouth University

About the authors

Natalie Bates is a research assistant at Bournemouth University and holds professional and academic qualifications in teaching and lifelong learning. Natalie's research focuses on the transfer of international social work skills and learning to the UK.

Elizabeth Burrow has worked with people receiving direct payments in a variety of settings since 1997. She completed her Diploma in Social Work (DipSW) in 2002 at Gloucestershire University. Since qualification, Elizabeth has worked within adult social care in a local authority in central England, primarily with adults with physical disabilities and older people. Elizabeth completed her PQ award in 2009.

Diane Galpin is a qualified social worker, having worked for 14 years in mental health, disability and older people services. She is currently a senior lecturer in post-qualifying social work at Bournemouth University and programme leader for the specialist award in Working With Vulnerable Adults.

Sally Lee began her career in the voluntary sector working with homelessness. After qualifying in 1993 with a DipSW and a Master's from Southampton University she has worked for local authorities, first in a hospital team for six years and then a rural team for older people. Sally now works in a small, very supportive team assisting adults with physical disabilities.

Emma Perry completed her Master's degree and DipSW at Keele University in 2004. Since then she has worked for a county council in the Midlands region in an older persons' team. She has undertaken a variety of roles in the team including duty worker and link worker for intermediate care. She is currently a GP-linked practitioner.

Jill Small has been a qualified social worker for 16 years. She has worked with people with learning disabilities for 26 years in a number of settings including her current post in a community team for people with learning disabilities. Jill has a special interest in adult protection work and has undertaken extensive post-qualifying training.

Acknowledgements

Social work practice occurs in an ever-changing and increasingly complex landscape. The role of practitioners in delivering adult social care is evolving and requires that individuals demonstrate a commitment not only to keeping up to date with changes at an organisational, policy and legislative level but also in developing new skills to ensure the highest professional standards.

Many social workers are now engaged in post-qualifying education as part of their commitment to social work and to improve practice with service users and carers. This involves a considerable amount of dedication, time and energy on the part of the practitioner, which the editors of this book salute.

This book has developed from the dedication of those qualified practitioners who have undertaken the Post-Qualifying Social Work Specialist Award in Social Work with Adults. The work of students who embark on the programme make up the core of this book and have heavily influenced the writing of other chapters.

The editors would like to thank those who have contributed to the book as authors, as well as the students and practitioners who have completed, or who are completing, their PQ studies, for their very hard work under what are sometimes difficult conditions.

Introduction

Aims and scope

This book is quite specific in its aim to provide a critical and analytical exploration of contemporary issues in social work with adults. It is not written to develop a consensus about what social work is or what practice should be, but rather to enable readers to expand their thinking, skills and knowledge beyond the point of their initial qualification: in essence to bring together academic learning and practice experience to facilitate professional development. This book does not include all areas of practice with adults as the framework for post-qualifying social work provides different routes for different areas of practice. The focus of content is, therefore, on the mainstream areas of older people and learning disability services – two of the larger service user groups in receipt of social care. These are also the service user groups from which most practitioners undertaking the Post-Qualifying Specialist Award in Social Work with Adults at Bournemouth University are drawn. This does not mean the debates raised throughout the book are exclusive to these groups alone, as issues of marginalisation, human rights, discrimination and oppression, for example, are pertinent to all those individuals social workers practise with and, in this sense, some of the observations, critiques and analysis from individual authors will be transferable across service user groups.

The core of this book, Chapters 2 to 5, are made up of some of the work that practitioners have written to meet the General Social Care Council's requirements for the Post-Qualifying Specialist Award in Social Work with Adults. All the work included is based on practitioners' experiences of practice. The first and last chapters provide an academic perspective, although still firmly rooted in experience of social work practice and the issues students bring to the programme.

Each chapter provides an analysis and critique of contemporary issues designed to stimulate debate and critical reflection for readers who are on their own post-qualifying journey. This book attempts to draw on practitioners' perspectives to facilitate learning for post-qualifying social work students. While not claiming to be the voice of all social workers, it provides a valid snapshot of some practitioners' experiences, which others may find useful.

Organisation of this book

The book is divided into six chapters. Each chapter provides a critical analysis of a specific area of practice identified by its author as relevant to social work and provides the reader with research and policy summaries, along with reflective activities that can be used at an individual level or within a team setting. The aim of the activities is to help practitioners step outside the day-to-day organisational context in which social work with adults occurs to reflect on their practice. This provides one way in which individuals can consolidate the skills and knowledge already used in practice and develop new skills and knowledge to improve practice and, ultimately, the experience for the service users and carers they work with.

Content of this book

Each chapter explores a different aspect of social work with adults, identifying issues that the authors suggest require debate and providing thoughts on how to develop professional practice.

Chapter 1 focuses on personalisation in the context of consumer rights and human rights. Policy and legislation from central government is committed to transforming social work with adults to ensure the development of social care services that are flexible, efficient, effective and economical.

Government is clear that the foundations of adult social care in the future will rest upon concepts such as personalisation, person-centred planning and choice. Practitioners are expected to facilitate reform across all service user groups by utilising practice tools, such as individual budgets and direct payment, to empower service users and carers to have more control over their lives in terms of assessment, care provision and management of care. This will mean a change of role for social work professionals as traditional tasks such as assessment and care management are transferred to others. However, practitioners and academics are beginning to question the veracity of the 'personalisation agenda' and wonder will all service users fit comfortably under the umbrella of 'personalisation'? If not, what will happen to those individuals?

Using a case study, Chapter 2 identifies the complex barriers that impact negatively on older people's lives, exploring the stereotypes that underpin society's view of older people and how social policy and legislation has attempted to address these to improve the lives of older people. Notions of independence and their meaning in terms of policy and practice are explored to highlight the somewhat one-dimensional view that policy and practice can support when working with older people. An overview of the legislative framework that supports practice with older people is identified to enable practitioners to develop anti-oppressive practice that is empowering yet does not undermine a statutory duty to protect individuals from abuse.

In Chapter 3 it is suggested that informal carers form the backbone of the British care system and as such are increasingly in the spotlight as their value to adult social care services is recognised. Caring can be viewed as both an activity and a disposition – something that is an integral part of being human and something we do, almost a natural response. Legislation and policy have developed to support carers in continuing with this important role; however, is this response being exploited to meet demographic concerns over an ageing population and the perceived increasing demand on limited resources in adult social care?

Political ideology underpinning policy and legislation pertaining to carers has been dominated over the last 20 years by neo-liberal perspectives that argue against state intervention and place much greater expectation upon individuals to develop networks of support that include informal carers. As the relationship between carers and the state changes under the auspices of modernisation, personalisation and transformation, what might this mean for informal carers?

Chapter 4 is made up of two parts. Part one provides an exploration of the context of practice in learning disability services from a policy and theoretical perspective, while part two looks at specific issues in practice by drawing on two case scenarios. Learning disability services is one of those areas of social work practice that has received much attention in terms of developing a system of assessment and provision built on the concept of personalisation. Policy has provided a welcome change of perspective as the focus of assessment has shifted to a person-centred approach.

However, the legislative context of practice is still embedded within the NHS and Community Care Act 1990. This chapter explores the links between community care and personalisation, providing an overview of critical debates within care management. Models of assessment and the care management process are suggested and offer useful practice lessons on which the process of personalisation can be built. Practice analysis is developed via two case studies to explore common themes in practice to help support practitioners develop their social work skills.

Chapter 5 explores direct payment in the context of working with older people, examining the socio-political context of their development and issues around the role of the social worker and risk. Direct payments are a cornerstone of contemporary practice, first developed successfully in physical disability services. In recent years, they have been extended to other service user groups with varying degrees of success. This chapter explores the barriers that may exist in the successful implementation within older persons' services and identifies concerns regarding the potential risks to those who use direct payments to develop their own personalised care pathway. The chapter concludes by presenting an anti-oppressive framework for practice and explores the implications of direct payments for older people in the future.

Chapter 6 explores the organisation and delivery of social work services across the United Kingdom, which has seen significant changes as government seeks to reform social care. Modernisation, personalisation and transformation (MPT) provide the structural frameworks that support social work practitioners in implementing reform. Social work should be thriving as a centralised 'one size fits all' approach gives way to an agenda premised on personalisation and transformation, where users of services are supported to take control of, and develop, their own personalised care pathways.

Research, however, would seem to suggest that social work is, at best, surviving rather than thriving under MPT. Chapter 6 critically analyses the context in which MPT has developed, suggesting an exploitation of ambiguity in meaning in policy and guidance, blended with a process of depoliticisation, has led to increasing disillusionment within the social work profession. While MPT appears congruent with the core values of social work, its implementation has been characterised by an individualistic approach to practice that obscures issues of structural discrimination and oppression, and reduces practitioners' consciousness of social work as a human rights activity. The chapter suggests the transformation of adult social care requires a commitment to human rights from both social work professionals and organisational leaders and a human rights-based approach to practice if social work is going to make a positive contribution to adult social care in the future.

Final thoughts

The overall aim in bringing this book together has been to add the voice of practitioners to current debates in social work with adults. Engagement by practitioners in post-qualifying social work education, whether as a student or lecturer, allows individuals to stop and reflect on practice and to ask difficult questions. This book presents some of their reflections and some of their questions.

Chapter 1

Personalisation: from consumer rights to human rights

Diane Galpin

ACHIEVING A POST-QUALIFYING SPECIALIST AWARD IN SOCIAL WORK WITH ADULTS

This chapter demonstrates how you might meet the GSCC specialist standards and requirements for post-qualifying social work education and training.

Legislation, social policy and social welfare

Social workers will need to extend and apply their knowledge and understanding of all relevant legal frameworks, social policies and social welfare principles within their particular area of practice. This includes all relevant legal and policy frameworks and the range of statutory responsibilities associated with working with adults. It also includes relevant legal and policy frameworks relating to mental health and the welfare of children and young people, together with the law relating to equality legislation and human rights.

Introduction

Social work practice with adults in the United Kingdom has undergone significant change as policy from central government over the last decade has focused on the modernisation of adult social care. Personalisation has been central to policy development in promoting self-directed and independent living for those eligible for services. It has also provided practitioners with an ideological framework on which to develop their practice focused on enabling those who use services to increase the level of choice and control they have over their own social care provision. Central to this approach has been the embedding of person-centred planning in practice to develop individualised responses to individual need supported by the development of individualised payments to those who use services from government in the form of personal budgets.

This chapter seeks to analyse the development and implementation of the personalisation agenda to explore whether while appearing to empower some users of services, personalisation also has the potential to undermine the protective frameworks that currently support practice with adults as rights become synonymous with consumer rather than human rights. Could personalisation increase marginalisation and compromise the human rights of those most vulnerable in society?

Background

ACTIVITY **1.1**

- *What do the terms 'modernisation' and 'personalisation' mean to you?*
- *What policy and legislation underpins the 'personalisation agenda'?*
- *How do these influence your practice?*

The organisation and delivery of social work services across the United Kingdom has seen significant change in the last decade. Two key strategies have underpinned this process: first, a shift in governmental responsibility from primary provider to regulator of services (Waine, 2000); and second, a greater emphasis on the role of service users, carers and the private and voluntary sector in transforming statutory service development (National School of Government, 2007). Leadbeater et al. (2008) suggest improving provision for those who use public sector services is dependent on utilising their skills and capacity to develop and manage self-directed health and social care pathways that transfer patterns of provision from the public to private sector and control from the professional to personal realm. To support these improvements, government has developed a strategy of modernisation and transformation built on the concept of personalisation. While England, Scotland, Wales and Northern Ireland have their own legislative and policy guidance, the concept of personalisation provides a framework for social work practice with adults in statutory services in the UK today.

ACTIVITY **1.2**

Team discussion – how does social policy relate to your practice?
Policy briefing: Modernising Social Services *(Department of Health, 1998a)*

This White Paper presented the new government's plans for modernising social services provision. It stated the principles underlying the government's 'third way' in relation to social care, which de-emphasised the status of the provider in favour of promoting independence and ensuring the delivery of quality services, and noted the establishment of a Social Services Modernisation Fund. The paper went on to outline proposals for improving services for adults and for children. It then set out proposals for general improvements in user protection, the system of regulation and workforce standards, and noted the intended establishment of the General Social Care Council. The paper's concluding sections explained plans for facilitating partnership with the NHS and non-statutory bodies, and presented a framework for cooperation between local authorities and central government in promoting the delivery of efficient, high-quality services.

ACTIVITY 1.2 (CONT.)

Key areas of particular concern included:

- *protection of adults exposed to neglect and abuse;*

- *coordination to ensure individuals were not left in hospital too long;*

- *inflexibility of service provision;*

- *clarity of role, the general public did not know who would provide services, what services were available or what standards could be reasonably expected;*

- *consistency, there was a huge difference in standards and levels of service between different local authorities that led to a general feeling of unfairness, christened in the media as the 'postcode lottery'.*

This White Paper provided a framework for government to develop subsequent policy and legislation used in practice today. Look at the key areas above and identify:

- *policy and legislation introduced since 1998 that seeks to address these issues.*

Discuss:

- *how successful these have been. (Where possible, identify any research that supports your evaluation.)*

Personalisation and social care reform

ACTIVITY 1.3

- *Produce a definition of personalisation – first, from a practice perspective, and, second, from a policy perspective.*

Hudson and Henwood (2008) suggest personalisation 'has developed from the social model of disability and the emerging ideology of independent living' (p18) that identified the barriers to achieving independent living that individuals with a disability faced. The report 'Improving the life chances of disabled people' (Prime Minister's Strategy Unit, 2005) acknowledged that individuals with a disability were all too often viewed as passive recipients of care and dependent on the services professionals decided they needed. The report also suggested an individual with a disability was more than able to identify their own needs and, furthermore, to identify the best way of meeting them. Therefore, a new approach was required to enable those with a disability to take control of their lives and live independently. The Green Paper *Independence, Well-being and Choice* (DH, 2005), followed by the White Paper *Our Health, Our Care, Our Say* (DH, 2006) and *Putting People First* (DH, 2007b), provided further guidance on the government's strategy of reform – to include the whole of adult service, not just those with a disability. These indicated that service provision should focus on a personalised approach that fitted service users' needs rather than the needs of statutory services (Hudson and Henwood, 2008).

The central theme of personalisation is one of choice. Foster et al. (2006) suggest personalisation focuses 'on the desired outcomes of service users. A commitment to assisting individuals to exercise choice concerning the types of services they prefer; collaborative and consultative decision-making processes; and funding arrangements that respond to, and uphold, the choices of service users, are core components of the personalised care approach' (p126). Personalisation begins with person-centred planning, which provides a holistic foundation for social work practice to support individuals in achieving choice. A person-centred approach begins by treating 'people as individuals with a unique history and personality, listens to their "voice" and recognises that all human life is grounded in relationships' (CSCI, 2009, p123).

Carr and Robbins (2009, p3) identify 'the introduction of individual or personal budgets as part of the wider personalisation agenda in adult social care' and, as such, enabling service users to achieve the choice(s) identified in a person-centred approach. For social work professionals in the UK, this has resulted in government developing specific policy and legislation to support practitioners in promoting personalisation; for example, direct payments and individual budgets (Manthorpe et al., 2008). Direct payments provide monies from the local authority to individuals in lieu of direct service provision (Glendinning et al., 2008) while 'individual budgets combine resources from different funding streams' (Carr and Robbins, 2009, p2); for example, community equipment services, Disabled Facilities Grants, Supporting People, Access to Work and the Independent Living Fund (Carr and Robbins, 2009). Individual budgets (IBs) build on the experiences of direct payment and In Control projects (Poll et al., 2006). Research suggests individuals have more choice and control in determining the type of support they require, how it will be delivered and by whom, when a personalised approach is used built on person-centred planning, direct payments and/or individual/personal budgets (Glendinning et al., 2008).

Personalisation, arguably, facilitates a participative approach which Leadbeater et al. (2008) suggest 'turns on its head traditional public service organisation. Traditional approaches put professionals at the centre of the process; participative approaches put the individual in charge' (p11). In the context of social care, Leadbeater et al. (2008) argue that by giving individuals their own budget they are able to develop the service solution that makes most sense to them.

Evidence suggests personalisation has benefited some service user groups. Research by Hatton et al. (2008) on person-centred planning with individuals with a learning disability suggests that this approach can provide real benefits to this service user group. Recent research from Glendinning et al. (2008), in their evaluation of an IB's pilot programme, suggests for those with mental health and physical disabilities, IBs appeared cost effective on social care and psychological well-being outcomes. However, for individuals with a learning disability results were mixed and for older people the evaluation states:

> *We found that older people were less likely than others to report higher aspirations as a result of the IB process. A statistically significant finding for older people suggested those in the IB group reported lower psychological well-being than those in the comparison group. (Glendinning et al., 2008, p19)*

Although reasons for this are not yet fully understood the extension of personalisation continues.

Policy briefing
The future of adult service provision is outlined in two key papers from government.

Our Health, Our Care, Our Say: a new direction for community services *(DH, 2006)*

This White Paper builds on the Green Paper Independence, Well-being and Choice *(DH, 2005) and states there will be a radical and sustained shift in the way services are delivered – ensuring they are more personalised and that they fit into people's busy lives. The paper outlined the government's agenda to increase direct payments to excluded groups with the introduction of individualised budgets and to develop a risk management framework to enable individuals to take greater control over decisions.*

Putting People First: a shared vision and commitment to the transformation of adult social care *(DH, 2007b)*

This protocol sets out the government's commitment to independent living for all adults, it also outlines the shared values and aims which will guide the transformation of adult social care, and it seeks to develop a collaborative approach between local and central government, the sector's professional leaders, providers and regulators to facilitate the development of a personalised system of adult social care.

Personalisation and marginalisation

Defining marginalisation
- *Marginalisation: being involuntarily disconnected from the economic and social mainstream of the society in which one lives; generally involves being discriminated against, being poor, having limited personal and collective power and being excluded from social opportunities.*

Marginalisation is a multi-layered concept linked to social status, it shifts as individuals move through their lives. Someone employed in a good job can become marginalised by unemployment. Similarly individuals can move through the life cycle in and out of marginal positions. Marginalisation is not just about being part of a 'minority'. For example, in South Africa, apartheid oppressed the black majority not the white minority. It is about an individual's proximity to powerful groups in control.

(Nelson and Prilleltensky, 2005)

Refer to this definition as you continue to the next activity.

The case for the continued extension of personalised services is argued in the report *Making it Personal* (Leadbeater et al., 2008, p1):

> *Personal budgets and self-directed services mobilise the intelligence of thousands of people to get better outcomes for themselves and more value for public money.*

5

The authors make bold claims to support the extension of personalisation arguing 'this participative approach delivers highly personalised, *lasting* solutions to people's needs for social care . . . at a lower cost than traditional, inflexible and top-down approaches' (Leadbeater et al., 2008, p9, authors' emphasis). The report later states 'our research shows that the most effective way to deliver on this commitment is to introduce self-directed services based on personal budgets' (p9), although the report does not clearly indicate what research it is referring to in relation to this statement. While Glendinning et al.'s (2008) evaluation may suggest that the positives of personalisation might be over-stated in some areas of practice, there is also a fundamental question one might ask regarding personalisation's ability to deliver a truly participative approach for all users of services.

Croft and Beresford (1996) discuss the 'paradox of participation' (p191), which might be pertinent in light of the above statements. They suggest while participation 'can be the route to redistributing power, changing relationships and creating opportunities for influence: equally it can double as a means of keeping power from the people and giving a false impression of its transfer' (p191). Personalisation in the shape of person-centred planning (PCP) might give such a false impression. For example, social work within learning disability services without PCP is 'inconceivable . . . PCP is often accepted without question as "a good thing"' (Le Mesurier et al., 2007, p3). However, Mansell and Beadle-Brown (2004) argue that there is a limited evidence base to its effectiveness and Le Mesurier et al. (2007) point to the ambiguity of the concept of PCP arguing 'the extent to which it is or can be applied to good effect at cost-effective levels is still far from clear' (p2).

Carey (2009) argues that service user and carer participation act as 'a mirage that conceal very different agendas' (p181), suggesting 'it fits with the principles of marketisation, especially the logic of consumerism and the implications of choice, engagement, participation, competitive tendering, and the like' (p183). One might wonder what will happen to those service users and carers identified as not benefiting from IBs (Glendinning et al., 2008) who are unable, or unwilling, to engage in this form of service user and carer participation. Scourfield (2007) suggests 'the consequences for those who "opt out" of personalised budget schemes such as Direct Payments have not been fully acknowledged' (p119). Could one answer be that this will result in social exclusion for some users of services as 'only those who are enterprising and can manage their own affairs will have earned the badge of citizenship' (Scourfield, 2007, p120)?

Leadbeater et al. (2008) recognise that not all people want individual budgets to purchase their own care provision; instead, they prefer traditional statutory services. Leadbeater et al. (2008) suggest local authorities will have to ensure provision to this *minority*; however, they also suggest 'closure and consolidation of local authority services is almost inevitable' (Leadbeater et al., 2008, p51). Leadbeater et al. (2008) does not identify who might make up the *minority* mentioned above; however, figures from National Statistics (2008) suggest around 1.23 million (69 per cent) of individuals receiving community care services in 2006–2007 were aged 65 and over. These make up the majority of service users in health and social care and therefore the *minority* may contain significant numbers of older people.

The use of the word 'minority' may hide more than it reveals. Possibly a more accurate description of these individuals might be 'marginalised' as they find themselves fitted into a system of personalisation whose foundations are firmly rooted in the experiences of service user groups primarily identified by their disability and whose life experiences, while arguably sharing similar inequalities, are not the same. The In Control model developed under the joint sponsorship of Mencap and the *Valuing People* Support Team began in 2003 founded on the key principle of enabling individuals with a disability to exercise their right to determine how to live independently (Hudson and Henwood, 2008). In Control has provided much of the basis for the personalisation agenda and the reform of adult services in England, yet the evaluation of In Control has not been conducted as large-scale formal research (Carr and Robbins, 2009). The first evaluation identified the positive potential for individuals with a learning disability. The second evaluation sought to identify if it might work with other adult service user groups; for example, physical disabilities and older people. However, over half the individuals included in the second study were people with a learning disability, and older people only made up 13 per cent of the total 196 participants. Carr and Robbins (2009) suggest the evaluation raised 'particular questions about operating self-directed support and personal budgets for older people' (p8).

The first step in a personalised approach to social work practice is PCP, as defined by Carr and Robbins (2009) above. This approach helps because older people are not a homogeneous group, being made up of individuals at varying stages of ageing and with varying levels of need. Anecdotal evidence, from social work practitioners, suggests that many of the 'older' older people they come into contact with (for example those aged over 85 who have spent their lives exercising choice and control in terms of working, home-making and raising a family) feel unable, or unwilling, to take on the responsibility of developing and managing individualised care pathways. Possibly unlike individuals with a learning disability who may never have had the opportunity, or permission, to take control and make choices in their lives.

This may be one reason why take-up of direct payments and IBs is lower among older service users (Carr and Robbins, 2009). Evaluations of schemes such as IBs identify that there are difficulties for older people (Carr and Robbins, 2009; Glendinning et al., 2008; Manthorpe et al., 2008); however, the focus following the identification of difficulties has been on simplifying systems or extending who might be able to manage say a direct payment for an older person, or suggestions that social work practitioners' limited knowledge of IBs and/or their low expectations of service users' abilities require attention, rather than acknowledging that for some older people IBs are just not an option.

Is it possible that the implementation of personalisation has become so focused on IBs that it would appear policy-makers believe one can only provide personalised services through IBs or a direct payment? If this is the case, modernisation might create a system that is just as inflexible as the one it is trying to replace: one that will marginalise those individuals who do not wish to engage in the financial aspects of personalisation.

ACTIVITY *1.4*

Read the research findings below and compare them to your practice experience

Research summary

Glendinning et al. (2008) *Evaluation of the Individual Budgets Pilot Programme*

This report provides an evaluation of the implementation of individual budgets (IBs). Thirteen local authorities were selected as pilot sites: two London boroughs, five metropolitan boroughs, four counties and two unitary authorities. The sample comprised of 959 people: 510 in the IB group and 449 in the comparison group (meaning they did not receive an IB). The distribution of the sample across service user groups were:

- *34 per cent working age with a physical disability;*

- *28 per cent older people;*

- *25 per cent learning disability;*

- *14 per cent working age mental health services.*

Outcomes

Physically disabled people: individuals from the IB group were more likely than the comparison group to report a higher quality of care and were more satisfied with the help they received.

Older people: reported lower psychological well-being than those in the comparison group. Information from interviews with service users and their proxies indicated many older people did not appear to want what many described as the 'additional burden' of planning and managing their own support.

People with learning disabilities: those in the IB group were more likely to feel they had control over their daily lives, although the difference was not statistically significant. Findings were particularly mixed for this group and readers should examine the full report to obtain a clearer understanding.

Mental health service users: those in the IB group reported significantly higher quality of life than those in the comparison group.

Another group of individuals at risk of marginalisation are self-funders. Hudson and Henwood (2008) highlight the inequity that exists in their review of eligibility criteria, suggesting there is some tension between the personalisation agenda and *Fair Access to Care Services* (FACS) (DH, 2002), stating that unless there are changes to FACS 'to bring a model of prioritisation more in line with that of personalisation, there will remain significant – and inappropriate – restrictions on the scope of self-directed support to achieve the ambitious objectives that are being set' (p23). They conclude in their overview of personalisation that it does not solve the problem of individuals who require support but are deemed ineligible, it also 'introduces some additional risks that certain groups of people may be marginalised' (p23).

ACTIVITY *1.5*

- *Re-read the definition of marginalisation.*

- *Having read this section, can you identify any areas where your service users and carers could feel marginalised?*

- *What can you do to ensure practice does not amount to marginalisation?*

Personalisation, discrimination and oppression?

ACTIVITY *1.6*

The relationship between discrimination and oppression
Thompson (2003) suggests that one of the main outcomes of discrimination is oppression. The relationship between discrimination and oppression can be seen as a causal one: discrimination gives rise to oppression.

Discrimination can be defined as:

> *Unfair or unequal treatment of individuals or groups; prejudicial behaviour acting against the interests of those people who characteristically belong to relatively powerless groups within a social structure.*

Oppression can be defined as:

> *Inhuman or degrading treatment of individuals or groups brought about by the dominance of one group over another: the negative or demeaning exercise of power. Oppression often involves disregarding the rights of an individual or group and is thus a denial of citizenship.*

Could personalisation lead to discrimination and oppression? Discuss.

For social work professionals, the marginalisation of individuals does not fit well with a value base built on a deontological approach to practice, where discrimination and oppressive outcomes are opposed (Waller, 2005). Yet the political context of practice today frequently compromises professionals' values and ethics, where a utilitarian approach to service delivery that focuses on outcomes for service users, especially in terms of cost effectiveness, is prevalent (Carey, 2009). From this perspective, personalisation is deemed neither good nor bad, but measured on whether it achieves more good than overall harm; for example, where only a 'minority' might experience the adverse effects of dismantling statutory provision.

An emphasis by government on what works (Jordan and Jordan, 2000) appears to support the marginalisation of those unable to participate in personalisation. Carey (2009) suggests there is a moral question to be answered when one considers the implementation by government of an approach 'that seeks to encourage service users and carers to integrate with, if not embrace, a political and economic system responsible for causing many of their problems' (p185).

Care as a commodity

For some commentators the focus of personalisation appears to be on modernising social care through a consumerist approach to services (Carey, 2009; Ramon, 2008) where Leece (2004) suggests 'social care provision is treated progressively as a commodity to be bought and sold' (p211). While Leadbeater et al. (2008) view this approach as encouraging a participatory approach, Clarke (2005) suggests this strategy is concerned with reducing costs to the state and enables government to meet 'neo-liberal concerns to "liberate" the citizen from the state' (p448). Both statements might be true and not necessarily in conflict with one another; however, both points of view are grounded in an economic approach to personalisation. As Bowers et al. (2007) suggests, when exploring person-centred planning with older people, it is not just about money. Yet anecdotal evidence from social work professionals suggests that this appears to underpin its implementation at a local level for many.

The problem of a consumerist approach to personalisation

The issue of economic rationality is central to a consumerist approach to personalisation and to the concepts of choice and control. Barnett (2006), exploring a social constructivist approach to international relations theory, suggests the concept of rational choice comes mainly from economic theory with an emphasis on the individual, or 'actor' (p267), and their ability to achieve their interests by using 'the most efficient means' (p267). Woods (2006) supports this view arguing in the context of international political economy that 'it is assumed that actors' interests and preferences are known or fixed and that actors can make strategic choices as to how best to promote their interests' (p335). Both Barnett (2006) and Woods (2006) suggest efficient and strategic choices are always made via the market. Choice in economic theory relates to exchanges between the individual and markets, with the markets being the most efficient means of meeting demand (Pratt, 2006). In the context of health and social care, these choices will be exercised through the service user and carer engaging in personalisation via schemes such as direct payments and individual budgets. In engaging in personalisation, the service user and carer are categorised as '*homo economicus* (rational, maximising agents)' (Le Grand et al., 2008, p71). The success of the personalisation agenda arguably relies on this premise. However, there are those in society who are unable, or unwilling, to be homo economicus and it is often with these individuals that practitioners' concerns around discrimination and oppression clash with the personalisation agenda.

There is a basic assumption within an economic approach to personalisation that the consumer knows their best interests better than anyone else; however, some consumers of health and social care do not possess the 'usual attributes of sound judgement and rationality that consumers are usually assumed to possess' (Le Grand et al., 2008, p55) – for example, through cognitive impairment. Of course a carer, family member or friend may act in an individual's best interest. However, this too might not be without problems as Le Grand et al. (2008) point out when discussing parents acting in the best interests of their children, suggesting there are times when parents do not act in the best interest of their children, especially where protection is an issue. The same argument might be applied to some adults dependent upon carers; for example, older people who do not have mental capacity.

Mansell et al.'s (2009) study of incidence of referrals, nature and risk factors in Adult Protection in two English local authorities may provide some support for Le Grand et al.'s (2008) suggestion. The study found a third (32 per cent) of all adult protection referrals were related to individuals living with their family, and 'the most frequently recorded types of abuse occurring in people's homes were physical abuse and financial abuse' (Mansell et al., 2009, p32). 'Half of all referrals relating to financial abuse were perpetrated by family members or carers' (Mansell et al., 2009, p33). The study also found 'those with mental health problems, those with disabilities and older people were more likely to experience abuse from families and carers (51 per cent, 61 per cent and 39 per cent, respectively) (Mansell et al., 2009, p33).

O'Keeffe et al.'s (2007) report into the prevalence of the abuse and neglect of older people found 2.6 per cent, 1 in 40, of older people over the age of 66 living in a private household reported experiencing 'mistreatment' from their partners or family members. Mistreatment was defined as physical, sexual and financial abuse, along with neglect. When neighbours and acquaintances were included the figure rose to 4 per cent. While not suggesting O'Keeffe et al.'s (2007) and Mansell et al.'s (2009) studies indicate there is a direct link between personalisation and adult abuse, it does, however, highlight how personalisation, in the form of IBs and direct payments, might increase the vulnerability of some service user groups to adult abuse when the focus of provision involves the support of family, who are unlikely to be regulated or monitored on a frequent basis.

Where best interest decisions are made on behalf of an individual by family and carers, is the system robust enough to ensure that, just as Le Grand et al. (2008) suggest some parents do not always act in their child's best interest, especially where protection is an issue, adults will not be left vulnerable to abuse? Section 146 of the Health and Social Care Act 2008 now makes it legal for more people to be made eligible for a direct payment 'by allowing other "suitable" people to consent and receive the payment on the disabled person's behalf' (Mandelstam, 2009, p53), including, in some circumstances, those users of service without mental capacity. Suitable people will include family or friends involved in providing care for an individual. Mandelstam (2009) suggests this increases risk to the individual, inferring in the context of a consumerist approach to social care that 'there may, however, be a tension between this notion of people as active consumers of social care services and safeguarding adults' (p54).

Another condition of rational choice requires consumers to be well informed so that they are able to evaluate the quality of the 'commodities they consume' (Le Grand et al., 2008, p180). However, research on the markets within the public sector in the areas of health care, education, housing and pensions suggests information falls short in supporting individuals to be well informed (Le Grand et al., 2008). This then does not allow the individual to make a rational choice as they are unable to weigh up the pros and cons accurately. Le Grand et al. (2008) suggests some individuals are unable to make rational decisions because 'individuals are subject to such extensive social and economic conditioning that they cannot make rational decisions concerning their consumption' (p181), linking this especially to the power of the media.

Human rights and personalisation

Human Rights Act 1998

The Human Rights Act is made up of 'articles'. Article 1 is an introduction and is not incorporated in the Act, the articles that apply in Britain are:

Article 2 – Rights to life

Article 3 – Prohibition of torture

Article 4 – Prohibition of slavery and forced labour

Article 5 – Right to liberty and security

Article 6 – Right to a fair trial

Article 7 – No punishment without law

Article 8 – Right to respect for private and family life

Article 9 – Freedom of thought, conscience and religion

Article 10 – Freedom of expression

Article 11 – Freedom of assembly and association

Article 12 – Right to marry

Article 13 – is not included in the HRA

Article 14 – Prohibition of discrimination

Article 16 – Restriction on political activity of aliens

Article 17 – Prohibition of the abuse of rights

Article 18 – Limitations on the use of restrictions on rights

(See A Guide to the Human Rights Act 1998, Department of Constitutional Affairs, www.dca.gov.uk.)

If the media does have the power Le Grand et al. (2008) suggest to shape public perception, one area of concern is human rights. The Human Rights Act 1998 has been the subject of attention in some sections of the media (*Daily Mail*, 2007) condemning it as a 'whingers' charter' (Mantell, 2008, p31), seeking its removal from public life. Yet, the extension of human rights is fundamental to ensuring those who engage in personalisation are not left outside any rights the Act confers.

The Human Rights Act (HRA) 1998 makes it unlawful for public authorities to act in breach of the fundamental rights and freedoms set out in the European Convention on Human Rights. Problems have arisen as original definitions of what constituted a 'public authority' were too narrow and excluded private and voluntary sector providers, leaving many individuals outside of the protection offered by the Act. This loophole has been partially addressed in the Health and Social Care Act (2008). Section 145 of the Act provides that individuals placed in an independent care/nursing home by a local authority are covered by the Human Rights Act 1998. To be covered, the service user must be placed in residential accommodation under Part III of the National Assistance Act 1948. However, section 145 does not confer human rights obligations on other independent care providers contracted by the local authority; therefore, independent domiciliary care agencies will continue to fall outside the Human Rights Act 1998 (Mandelstam, 2009). This amendment also does not address the issue of individuals who receive publicly arranged social care in their own home; for example, by personal assistants employed under direct payments or as part of an individual budget. Therefore, working in a manner consistent with human rights in an individual's home is left to the discretion of the provider.

The British Institute of Human Rights (BIHR) (2008) suggest that individuals receiving care services in their own homes are vulnerable to abuse. The BIHR argue that 'those who remain outside of the HRA have no direct legal remedy under the Act against those providing care. Consequently, they are unable to directly challenge these shocking abuses as violations of their human rights' (p3). The potential impact on the quality of care provided by these individuals is made explicit when the BIHR states 'of equal importance is the fact that these providers are not given any encouragement to develop a culture of respect for the human rights of their vulnerable service users' (2008, p3).

The Commission for Social Care Inspectorate (CSCI) (2008) has identified the 'variability in the quality of support provided to individuals who experience abuse, which is unacceptable given that abuse is a violation of a person's human rights' (p3). CSCI suggests 'more needs to be done to ensure people who direct their own support on a daily basis are also able to benefit from appropriate and individually tailored safeguards' (p3).

Scourfield (2007) asks a pertinent question when writing about 'building a welfare system around the entrepreneurial individual' (p119) – 'with the public sector relieved of more of its responsibilities, how will it ensure social justice in those situations?' (p120). The same question might be asked for the human rights of those engaged in personalisation in their own homes through the use of schemes such as IBs and direct payments. While the exclusion of individuals receiving care in their own homes under such schemes has never been subject to human rights, what is different is the government's aim to include those service users who have been excluded in the past; for example, those without mental capacity can have someone act in their best interest. This is to be welcomed; however, it also needs to be acknowledged that practitioners may be removing these individuals from one mode of care provision that supports the protection of their human rights in law, into a system where they are no longer protected under human rights law. Ife (2008) states that from a human rights perspective acting in someone's best interest 'can easily become itself a human rights violation' (p173), going on to suggest from a practitioner's perspective it 'must be undertaken only with a sense of deep unease and moral questioning' (p173). The same might be asked of those from outside the profession who take on this responsibility on behalf of those service users who are unable to.

ACTIVITY **1.7**

Team discussion

Healy (2008), in an analysis of the history of social work as human rights profession, suggests 'it is fair to conclude that social workers have usually paid more attention to human needs rather than to human rights' (p745).

- *Do you agree or disagree with this statement? If so, why?*

Healy (2008) continues, suggesting 'Social workers take action; they engage in securing rights for individuals and communities. What is missing, perhaps, is a consciousness of the activities of social work as human rights practice and of ways to build on individual case solutions to influence policy change' (p746).

- *How does your practice interact with human rights?*

- *Identify examples of good practice.*

- *What barriers might exist to developing human rights-based social work practice?*

- *How can you remove these barriers?*

Newman (2007) suggests privatisation is a 'new form of governmental power in which the personal becomes both an object (of new strategies) and a resource (to be mobilised in the process of constituting new forms of self-governing welfare subjects)' (p365). Might the same be said of personalisation as care provision is increasingly located outside statutory services and their protective frameworks; for example, human rights? It remains to be seen what frameworks of knowledge and skills might support a personalised service. Omission of knowledge pertaining to human rights may prove a serious oversight as ethical considerations are weakened and hard won recognition of the levels of abuse, oppression and discrimination experienced by service users and the development of protective services are lost in the drive for personalisation.

A system of care provision that both empowers and protects should be built on more than accepting personalisation is always 'a good thing' and economic notions of rational choice, where clear boundaries between consumer and human rights are blurred. The modernisation of social care through personalisation requires well-informed users of services who are able to choose if they wish to resist a strategy that promises so much in terms of promoting inclusion but may just as easily promote exclusion and disadvantage (Carey, 2009) if service users and carers engage as entrepreneurs (Scourfield, 2007) in a consumerist, rather than personalised, system of welfare provision. Could personalisation lead to a two-tier system of care provision where some users of services are entitled to legal rights, as conferred under the Human Rights Act 1998, while others are excluded in the name of consumer rights?

Chapter summary

- Social work practice with adults in the United Kingdom has undergone significant change over the last decade as policy from central government has focused on the modernisation of adult social care.

- Personalisation has been central to policy development in promoting self-directed and independent living for those eligible for services. It has also provided practitioners with an ideological framework on which to develop their practice focused on enabling those who use services to increase the level of choice and control they have over their own social care provision.

- The positives of personalisation might be overstated in some areas of practice. There is also a fundamental question one might ask regarding personalisation's ability to deliver a truly participative approach for all users of services.

- There is a basic assumption within an economic approach to personalisation that the consumer knows their best interests better than anyone else; however, some consumers of health and social care do not possess the essential attributes to make a rational choice – for example, mental capacity.

- The Human Rights Act 1998 does not apply to independent domiciliary care agencies. Therefore, individuals who receive publicly arranged social care in their own home – for example, by personal assistants employed under direct payments or as part of an individual budget – are not protected by human rights.

- Social work should be viewed as human rights practice.

FURTHER READING

Ife, J. (2008) *Human rights and social work: towards rights-based practice.* Melbourne: Cambridge University Press.

This book outlines the role of human rights in supporting social work practice and suggests that framing social work as a human rights profession can enable practitioners to view practice dilemmas in a new light by providing a moral base for practice while helping to support the development of social policy.

Chapter 2

Working with older people: managing risk and promoting interdependence

Emma Perry

Introduction

Social work with older people is often seen as routine, uninteresting and less complex than work with children (Thompson, 2006) and other adults. This rather simplistic and discriminatory view fails to acknowledge the variety of needs that older people have and the wide range of factors which impact on them.

This chapter will explore some of the issues that influence social work practice with older people, focusing on the areas of policy and legislation, risk, mental capacity, dependence and interdependence, power and resources. Consideration will be given to the ageing process and how this is portrayed in society. A case study will be used to develop the discussion to identify and address issues faced by social workers who work with older people.

Challenging views on the ageing process

Many older people who come into contact with social services do so as a result of difficulties arising as part of the ageing process, that is, deterioration in physical health and/or cognitive impairment. Approaches to this stage of life typically focus upon these changes and therefore tend to view old age as a period of unavoidable decline arising from a loss of functioning. However, seeing old age in these terms is incredibly one-dimensional and arguably leads to the perpetuation of ageism. Interpreting ageing as a biological event alone might be viewed as a form of discrimination (Bytheway and Johnson, 1990, cited in Thompson, 2006, p111).

The predominance of this view of growing old can have a considerable impact on older people. For the individual, signs of ageing become something to be feared as ageing becomes associated with frailty and incapacity. 'Problems' of old age become medicalised and therefore legitimised and accepted while the ways in which older people adapt to these changes and experience the ageing process is overlooked. Focusing upon the biological changes in ageing also results in what Thompson (1994, cited in Thompson, 2003, p27) terms 'naturalisation', as old age becomes seen as a time of natural decline and withdrawal from society. Through this process older people become portrayed in an unnecessarily negative manner, a culture evolves where ageist assumptions go unquestioned and certain behaviours and situations become viewed as 'normal' for particular groups of people. These elements result in the emergence of ageist beliefs and ideology. At a structural level this essentialist approach to ageing becomes a justification for inequality and acts as a substantial barrier to change.

Over the past two decades, the policy approach from central government has sought to change this view of the ageing process. Prior to the community care reforms of the early 1900s, policy was in keeping with Cumming and Henry's (1961, cited in Gross, 1996, p617) 'disengagement theory'. Old age was viewed negatively, older people were seen as a burden and later life was seen as a distinct and separate life stage governed by different needs. The provision of residential care can be seen as a way of assisting older people to

disengage from society. In contrast, current government thinking appears to be taking more of an activity theory approach to ageing. Recent policies emphasise that quality of life and well-being can be improved through access to leisure, social activities and active participation in the community (e.g., DH, 2005) and there are moves away from providing services on the basis of age (e.g., DH, 2001a, 2002).

Despite this being a more positive view, several criticisms can be made, namely policies and procedures tend to provide a prescriptive approach that only sees an idealised vision of growing old. Older people are presented as a homogeneous group with similar needs and there is a failure to recognise that not everyone is able to exercise choice over how they age or if they remain active. There is also little acknowledgement within policy of the role of wider political, social or economic factors and a failure to consider the experiences of marginalised and minority groups of older people or the role of stigma and oppression in their lives.

Practice analysis

CASE STUDY 2.1

Mrs Ensor is 88 years old and has been diagnosed with dementia. She lives with her husband who is her main carer. Mr Ensor tends to lack insight into his wife's requirements and there have been two incidences in the past where he has failed to seek medical attention for her when needed. Last year Safeguarding Adults procedures were initiated for this reason following a hospital admission.

Several weeks ago Mrs Ensor was admitted to an Intermediate Care Unit following deterioration in her mobility.

The Ensor's daughter, Tracey, has a very poor relationship with her father and feels very strongly that her mother should not be at home with him. She has made several claims that her father neglects her mother.

Dependence and independence

Old age is a time that is strongly associated with increased dependency and a reduction in independence. As a result of the predominance of the medical/biological approach to ageing, this is typically seen in physical terms. Dependence therefore comes to be seen as inherently negative and to be avoided at all costs, while independence is something that must be preserved and maintained. This view of dependence reinforces notions of older people as 'burdens', portrays them in a powerless position and tends to lead to the over-simplification of a complex range of factors surrounding old age (Thompson, 2006). It also fails to acknowledge that dependency, and to a certain extent independence, is a complex and multi-faceted issue (Fine and Glendinning, 2005).

One of these complexities becomes apparent when considering cases such as Mrs Ensor. While she is physically reliant upon her husband, it could be argued that she is also dependent upon him in an emotional/psychological and financial sense. There is therefore much more to dependency than just the physical; it can take many different forms that extend beyond just a personal level. Additionally, the different types of dependency do not exist in isolation; rather, they interact with each other and exacerbate the effects of age-related disabilities (Wenger, 1986, cited in Fine and Glendinning, 2005, p606). The negative and limited way in which dependency has become viewed also ignores the important fact that it is actually a normal and necessary social condition (Fine and Glendinning, 2005). It is effectively how dependency has been constructed within society and policy that results in some types being accepted while other forms are seen as undesirable.

In addition to viewing dependency as a social and ideological construct, it can also be considered at a structural level. A 'structured dependency' approach emphasises how dependency is created or increased among older people as a result of political, social and economic conditions. The welfare state and social services are included within this (Townsend, 1981; Walker, 1982, both cited in Tanner and Harris, 2008, p34; Thompson, 2006). Research has found that staff in residential care settings often over-help older people and create dependency (Hagestad and Uhlenberg, 2005), while Walker and Walker's (1998) work into older people with learning difficulties highlights how once people reach 65 and move into older people's services, the emphasis changes from independence to care with dependency almost being expected and indirectly reinforced. It may be argued that by providing Mrs Ensor with a homecare service, the social worker effectively legitimised and highlighted her dependency on state-provided support, while the tendency for social services eligibility criteria to focus upon functional skills/daily tasks may be seen to be increasing reliance upon others among the older population and reinforcing the negative and limited view of dependency.

Independence, like dependence, can be defined in a number of different ways. Older people tend to view it in much wider terms than professionals and highlight that it can involve issues around choice and maintaining a meaningful social identity and role (Sixsmith, 1986, cited in Secker et al., 2003 p378). In recent years, there has been a move towards considering independence in relation to having choice and control over the care and support that is required, what has been termed 'decisional autonomy'. The government has adopted this approach in *Independence, Well-being and Choice* (DH, 2005) and it is the underlying principle behind the recent personalisation agenda of *Transforming Social Care* (DH, 2008a) and *Putting People First* (DH, 2007b).

This view of independence and the changes that are forthcoming in social care appear very positive; however, it is not without difficulties. The personalisation of social care is built on the basis of service users being able to participate in the system. While this might pose no problem to the majority of service users, there are still a significant number of older people, like Mrs Ensor, who have cognitive impairments and may find it difficult to exercise choice even with support and advocacy. Given the numbers of older people who experience illnesses such as dementia, it may be argued that a significant amount of this service user group will be marginalised and excluded from the new systems and developments in social care. For these individuals personalisation may be seen as a further example of structured dependency.

Although practitioners are unable to change the direction that government policy takes, it is possible to adopt an anti-oppressive and empowering view of older people while working within it. This can be done through thinking in terms of interdependence with older people rather than the opposing notions of independence and dependence. Interdependence as a concept implies a more equal exchange and balance of power and recognises the reciprocal nature of caring arrangements. Most importantly, rather than seeing the cared-for person as a burden, it acknowledges their role and the contribution that they make and also allows us to recognise that the person who is the carer is likely to have needs of their own. For example, while Mrs Ensor needs her husband to meet practical and emotional needs, he also requires support and gains from this situation. I believe that caring for his wife gives Mr Ensor a role and his life purpose while the actual task of providing care keeps him occupied throughout the day and gives him a much needed routine. Interdependence therefore enables older people who require support to be perceived in a more positive light and allows a much more accurate reflection of the complexity of human and caring relationships in later life.

The concept of interdependency can also be useful when considering services for older people. It was discussed previously how social care for older people tends to create dependency; however, direct payments can be seen as a much needed exception. This type of provision is heralded as increasing independence as people are given choice and control, yet I would argue that it is more accurate and empowering to think of direct payments in terms of interdependency. While service users may rely upon their personal assistants, the employment basis of their relationships means that the latter is dependent upon the service user financially as they rely upon them for work. Direct payments are therefore a key example of interdependency as it creates reciprocal relationships and effectively gives older people power rather than removes it from them.

Research summary

Secker et al. (2003) provide a two-dimensional model to help conceptualise independence at an individual level, thus providing a useful tool to support a person-centred approach to assessing the meaning of independence to the individual rather than restrict its meaning to the parameters of policy and legislation. The research found older people conceptualised independence in much broader terms, so that even where individuals had high levels of physical dependence they perceived themselves as independent because they included aspects such as self-esteem, self-determination, purpose in life and personal growth.

For further reading see Secker et al. (2003).

Power and oppression

Previous discussions around ageist beliefs and structured dependency highlight how frequently older people occupy positions of relative powerlessness within society. Age is a social division and a crucial factor when considering the allocation of power, opportunity, privilege and social roles (Thompson, 2003, 2006). It has been claimed that older people are among the most disempowered of the population (Jack, 1995a cited in Thompson, 2006, p103). This is likely because they do not just face discrimination on the basis of age. Older people experience multiple oppressions – for example, for Mrs Ensor this is likely to be as a result of her mental health diagnosis and gender, in addition to her age – and inequalities such as poverty that are experienced earlier in the life-course tend to continue into old age.

Power is a very complex issue and it should not be thought of in terms of an object, something that people either do or do not possess. As Vincent (1999) explains, 'power is embedded in a pre-existing structure of relationships and it is this power that enables some definitions to be more readily accepted than others' (p15). People who are in positions of power can present their construction of the world in ways that protect and consolidate their position, at the expense of the less powerful. Ageist ideology is a central mechanism in this construction that places older people at a disadvantage. The structural nature of power relations becomes apparent when considering situations where older people have gained a small amount of power through service user participation. They have not only highlighted issues around services but also identified problems with the political, economic, strategic and structural elements of established organisations (Carr, 2007).

Power dynamics and oppression are therefore rooted in the very structure of society. Biggs (1993) highlights how the models employed by policy-makers are based upon assumptions that put older people in a passive relationship to social policy. It has been suggested that recent policy is constructing a new set of expectations around growing old and 'successful ageing' is now being defined as the continuation of middle-aged activities such as work and work-like activities, that is, volunteering for as long as possible (Biggs et al., 2008). Criticisms of this activity theory approach in policy have already been made, yet Biggs et al. (2008) raise another important point that this 'blurring of the life-course' rather than freeing older people from age discrimination may actually create a new form as differences in aspirations, parts of the life-course and the physical realities of later life are ignored. By trying to re-define later life, policy is actually denying the special qualities and attributes of growing old.

A further consequence of this new view of old age is a fragmentation among older people. Individuals who are 'third age' older people and are active and independent are able to participate in society, engage with the political agenda of *Independence, Wellbeing and Choice* (DH, 2005) and *Our Health, Our Care, Our Say* (DH, 2006) and embrace personalisation. In contrast, 'fourth age' older people who are dependent and frail are likely to be excluded and disadvantaged. This is significant as it is older people in this latter group who are likely to be the most disempowered and make up the majority of social care service users.

In addition to power relations at a structural level, social workers also need to have an understanding of how power dynamics operate on an individual level. As stated above, social work is typically undertaken with those who are disadvantaged and hold least power in society. Practitioners, because of their professional status, knowledge and control over access to resources and statutory powers (although it may be argued that this latter element is much reduced in work with adults compared to children's services), inevitably occupy a position of much greater power than service users. Workers therefore need to be aware of this, how they can be perceived by service users and that all power, regardless of who possesses it, is open to abuse (Beckett and Maynard, 2005). Professionals need to ensure that the power that they hold is used for the benefit of service users rather than to further disempower or disadvantage. This can be achieved through upholding social work values around protecting, promoting and respecting the rights of service users and being accountable for their practice (GSCC, 2002). Practitioners should also be open and honest with service users and work in an empowering way. Empowerment can take many different forms (Banks, 2006).

Practitioner reflections

I feel that my own practice tends to be concerned with empowerment at an individual level through ensuring that older people have choice, can exercise their rights and have their voice heard, rather than the more radical approach of bringing about change at a societal level.

ACTIVITY 2.2

How do you ensure that your professional practice exercises the use of power in a non-oppressive manner?

One of the key ways in which power relations can be played out at an individual level is through the use of language. This is where 'meanings are shaped and contested, identities formed and challenged' (Thompson, 2003, p55). Language can be used as a means to express power and status. Jargon, for example, has a tendency to create barriers and can be used to exclude people. This is an important issue for practitioner and service user relationships, but applies equally to multi-disciplinary working, where language can be used by some professionals to try to assert power and authority over others. Thompson (2006) highlights how medical discourse reflects the power of the medical profession and contributes to the perpetuation of this power.

Practitioner reflections

The social work team I work in is due to become integrated and we will be joined by two workers who are trained nurses, employed by the health service. While I feel that the addition of their skills and knowledge will benefit the team enormously, I also expect there to be differences in opinion and possible power struggles. It is likely that these struggles will be played out in the use of professional language and there are likely to be some interesting discussions.

Resources and inequality

The area of resources is very closely linked to the issue of power. The amount of resources that different groups are given can be seen as a reflection of their worth or importance within society and older people and their carers are frequently a low priority when it comes to service provision (Thompson, 2006). It has been suggested that one of the central causal factors of this is the emphasis upon economics and the importance attributed to work within society (Phillipson, 1982, cited in Thompson, 2006, p110). This has resulted in people being viewed as commodities and valued by their potential productivity levels. On these terms, older people have little to contribute and are seen as having little social or economic value.

The provision of services for older people in the social care sector does appear to reinforce this notion. Despite being covered by the same community care legislation, older people are not able to access the same level of services as their counterparts who come under the remit of physical disability or learning disability teams. Many county councils operate a 'net cost policy' within older peoples' services, which is based upon the principle that it should not cost more for an older person to remain at home rather than enter residential care, which severely limits the amount of resources that older people can receive. This is despite the recommendations contained within *Fair Access to Care Services* (FACS) (DH, 2002). However, this may change in the future with the requirement for costings to become more transparent under the personalisation agenda and the intended Equality Bill may necessitate some changes in the way in which services are structured and delivered (Community Care, 2008).

Inequality at a structural level inevitability impacts upon inequality at a personal level. When considering material resources, older people are over-represented at the bottom of society (Vincent, 1999), one in four single older women live in poverty (Age Concern, 2003 cited in Tanner and Harris, 2008, p20) and older people are more likely to experience persistent poverty (Price, 2006). Significant amounts of this age group are socially excluded as a result of having low incomes and living in poor neighbourhoods (Scharf and Phillipson, 2004, cited in Biggs et al., 2008, p244). It is, however, vital to acknowledge that age does not bring these differences and they should not be considered in isolation. Older people's situations reflect the social inequalities of class, gender and race in the society in which they have lived (Vincent, 1999). Differences and inequalities experienced earlier in the life course continue and are exacerbated by the effects of ageing.

Older people's financial resources are an area that, over recent years, has increasingly impacted upon social work practice. Because of limited resources and tightening eligibility criteria, practitioners now have to establish an older person's financial situation before they are able to arrange services. Arguably this has resulted in the development of a two-tier system in social care as those who qualify for state support and those who are 'self-funding' are required to take different pathways to obtain services. While it may be seen that the latter are placed at an advantage as they usually have more choice, control and are able to arrange services quickly, there are also numerous disadvantages associated with arranging your own care (CSCI, 2008). The issue of finances was considered in the case of Mrs Ensor. When her care package was set up, Mr Ensor did not wish to divulge details of his wife's finances and this resulted in her being charged the full cost. After several months he attempted to cancel some of the calls because of cost concerns. A reduction in her package would have had an influence on how risks were being reduced and her well-being managed. Therefore, the social work practitioner and manager then had to exercise professional discretion to balance issues of protection and autonomy. In this case it led to a cap being placed upon her charges and the local authority had to meet part of the cost of the care package. This ensured Mrs Ensor remained where she most wanted to be, at home, and reduced the likelihood of her being at risk at home.

Working with risk

ACTIVITY 2.3

Carson and Bain (2008) suggest risk assessment involves two variable factors that need to be taken into consideration when making a decision about risk:

- *outcomes;*

- *likelihood.*

In this case scenario, what potential outcomes can you identify and what is the likelihood of these happening? How might you then use these answers to develop a risk management strategy?

One of the central issues in social work with adults is a concern with the identification and management of risk. In the above case scenario, the ongoing adult protection concerns and claims made by the daughter would mean the social worker would need to ensure frequent re-examination of the potential risks to Mrs Ensor; for example, whether she should remain at home in the care of her husband. While the daughter might feel strongly that Mrs Ensor should be somewhere where she would be 'safe and looked after' rather than at home with her father, the social worker's views on what might be an 'acceptable' level of risk could be quite different.

It is necessary to work with and consider the opinions of family members; however, if the social worker were to accept the daughter's views without critical analysis of the whole situation, this could result in a very protectionist and oppressive stance. In order to avoid this, the social worker would need to try to focus upon exactly what the risks to Mrs Ensor are and the potential impact upon her through completing a Person-Centred Risk Assessment and Management Plan (from Titterton, 2005). This would enable the worker to address the daughter's concerns while keeping a balanced view of the risks and acknowledging the positive aspects of Mrs Ensor being at home. The social worker should also ensure they demonstrate how any risks would be managed; for example, through the provision of a home care package. In this case, a critically analytical approach in risk assessment revealed that on occasions there was no support for some of the daughter's claims. For example, she repeatedly stated that her father did not give her mother enough to eat, but regular checks by the district nurses revealed that Mrs Ensor's weight remained stable.

Risk assessment and management is a key element and crucial issue in social work with older people (Hughes, 1995; Ray and Phillips, 2002). When working in this area, practitioners need to be highly aware of the role of ageism and the impact of cultural beliefs. This applies in two separate but interrelated areas: older people's self-perception and the views held by relatives and professionals. Research has found that older people themselves can often hold negative attitudes and accept stereotypes of ageing (Minichiello et al., 2000; Fenge, 2001), which can lead to a sense of increased dependency and loss of self-esteem (Marshall, 1990). This can then become a self-fulfilling prophecy as once older people believe that they are no longer independent, contributing adults, they come to adopt a passive dependent role (Butler et al., 1991, cited in Nelson, 2005, p210), which in turn reinforces ageist stereotypes (Grant, 1996). The result of this is that older people can come to accept that younger people can make decisions for them, autonomy can be reduced and choice and risk removed from their lives (Wynne-Harley, 1991, cited in Titterton, 2005, p19).

Carers and relatives of service users, along with professionals, may also have their views influenced by ageist beliefs. It could be argued in this case that the daughter may have been taking a paternalistic welfarist approach to her mother's care on the basis of her age and mental health diagnosis.

Research summary

Research has found that age and gender stereotypes lead to inconsistencies in social attitudes towards risk – people are generally more tolerant towards risk-taking behaviour in younger people, especially males (Orme, 2001, cited in Tanner and Harris, 2008, p191).

Practitioners need to be aware of these factors and how they may influence decision-making, particularly as this is likely to happen on a subconscious level as a result of negative notions of older people being part of the 'taken-for-grantedness of everyday life' (Thompson, 2003, p21). Thompson (2006) warns that workers 'must be wary of allowing ageist ideology to tilt the balance in favour of an over-cautious, perhaps somewhat paternalistic, approach' (p109).

It is inarguably the case that values are inextricably linked to risk analysis and are of central importance in risk management (Parrott, 2006). The more a paternalistic view is taken to risk and older people, the more this impinges upon their rights to self-determination, dignity, self-worth and respect. However, given the findings discussed above around older people holding and internalising negative views, the practitioner needs to go beyond just protecting and respecting individuals' rights required by professional ethics (GSCC, 2002). They need to ensure that decisions that older people make are based upon accurate information and are fully informed while also being aware of the role that ageist ideology may be having on decision-making.

While these elements impact upon an individual level, it is important to acknowledge that there are significant changes in the way in which risk is being constructed at a structural level that will also shape and influence social work practice. Today's society is increasingly focused upon risk (Beck, 1992, cited in Titterton, 1999, p220) and it is an issue that has become increasingly 'individualised and responsibilised' (Kemshall, 2002, p1). Risk has evolved from something that happens externally as a result of accident or fate into being perceived as an issue of choice and something that can be controlled or avoided. This shift is reflected in recent policy which moves away from a paternalistic approach towards a more rights-based model (e.g., DH, 2005, 2007a; CSCI, 2006). While this is positive and corresponds more closely with anti-oppressive practice and social work values, we are still a long way from society accepting that older people still have the right to take risks. Ageist attitudes and beliefs are so embedded within society that for any change to be successful a significant cultural shift and change in ideology is required and this is likely to take a considerable time to achieve.

Using policy and legislation to underpin practice

> ### ACTIVITY 2.4
>
> - *Write a list of policy and legislation that you might use to support your work in a case such as Mrs Ensor's.*
>
> - *What is your understanding of the purpose of each item on your list?*

There are several pieces of policy and legislation that practitioners can draw on to support practice that both empowers and protects individuals such as Mrs Ensor. While not exhaustive, the following section provides an overview of some key policy and legislation that practitioners should be using.

Human Rights Act 1998

In October 2000, the Human Rights Act came into effect in the UK. This means individuals could take cases regarding breaches of their human rights into a court in the UK. There are 16 basic rights in the Human Rights Act which cover concerns such as matters of life and death, freedom from torture along with rights around what a person can say or do, or a right to a fair trial. Practice undertaken by professional social workers should be compatible with the Human Rights Act 1998 (see 'Making sense of human rights; a short introduction' at **www.justice.gov.uk/docs/hr-handbook-introduction.pdf**).

> ### *The Human Rights Act 1998 and practice*
> *The role of Best Interest Assessor under the Mental Capacity Act (2005) Deprivation of Liberty Safeguards has developed to address breaches of Article 5 of the Human Rights Act 1998. The foundations of this legislation are firmly embedded in the protection of individuals' human rights.*

HL v UK 2005: The 'Bournewood Gap'

HL has a learning disability and is unable to speak. His level of understanding is limited. He has a history of self-harm and frequently becomes agitated. He has been in the care of Bournewood Hospital for many years; however, for the last three years has successfully resided with paid carers. In July 1997 while at the day centre, he is very agitated and harms himself. Staff are unable to contact the paid carers so contact a local doctor who administers a sedative. He remains agitated, is taken to accident and emergency, and eventually returns to Bournewood Hospital as an informal patient (opposed to being admitted under the Mental Health Act 1983). HL's carers were unable to visit or remove HL from hospital and eventually went to court to gain access to him. They eventually saw him again for the first time since his admission in November 1997. Following several court cases, the European Court decide that HL has been deprived of his liberty while an 'informal' patient and that this breached Article 5 of the Human Rights Act 1998.

National Service Framework

The National Service Framework (NSF) for Older People (DH, 2001a) provides practitioners with an ethical foundation on which to build anti-discriminatory and anti-oppressive practice as it outlines the government's agenda to improve practice standards within health and social care when working with older people.

The NSF sets standards for the care of older people across health and social services. These standards apply whether an older person is being cared for at home, in a residential setting, or in a hospital.

The NSF focuses on:

- rooting out age discrimination;
- providing person-centred care;
- promoting older people's health and independence;
- fitting services around people's needs.

The NSF should provide one of the foundations on which good social work practice with older people is built.

Safeguarding Adults

Safeguarding Adults: A Study of the Effectiveness of Arrangements to Safeguard Adults from Abuse

A survey has estimated that 227,000 older people have experienced neglect or abuse by persons they should have been able to trust. Sharp rises in the number of people who are over 85 years old would suggest this figure might rise and, indeed, given the numbers of very elderly people with conditions such as dementia who often find it more difficult to report abuse, might well be an underestimate. (CSCI, 2008, p16)

Safeguarding Adults (ADSS, 2005) provides a national framework of standards for good practice and outcomes in adult protection work. The framework is comprised of 11 sets of good practice standards which support adult protection policy and procedures in practice. These are part of a complex framework of policy and legislation used in the protection of vulnerable adults. *No Secrets* (DH, 2000) provides policy guidance on identifying adult abuse and how health and social care organisations and practitioners should engage in adult protection. Both *Safeguarding Adults* and *No Secrets* should be used by practitioners in conjunction with a number of pieces of legislation available to support the protection of vulnerable adults.

These include:

- *the law and physical abuse* – Offences Against the Persons Act 1861 (s.39, s47, s18 and s20), Criminal Law Act 1967 (s4(1), s17, s24, s25), Medicines Act 1968 (s58);

- *the law and sexual abuse* – Sexual Offences Act 2003 (s1–s4, s30–s37, s39–s42, s66 and s67);

- *the law and financial abuse* – Theft Act 1968, Fraud Act 2006 (s1, s4(1), s8, s21);

- *the law and emotional abuse* – Protection from Harassment Act 1997 (s2);

- *the law and neglect* – Mental Capacity Act 2005 (s44), National Health Services Act 2006 (s254 and Sch 20), National Assistance Act 1948 (s47), National Assistance (Amendment) Act 1951;

- *the law and discriminatory abuse* – Race Relations Act 1976, Sex Discrimination Act 1975, Disability Discrimination Act 1995, Crime and Disorder Act 1998 (s28–s32, s82), Racial and Religious Hatred Act 2006, Forced Marriage (Civil Protection) Act 2007;

- *the law and institutional abuse* – Care Standards Act 2000;

- *the law and domestic violence* – The Domestic Violence, Crime and Victims Act 2004.

Knowledge of the law is extremely important in practice but frequently it is marginalised by other factors such as internal policies and procedures. While these remain important, the law is integral to social work practice and provides a foundation on which to build good practice with vulnerable adults.

> *Appropriate use of adult protection procedures should ensure that, just as any other citizen of this country, a vulnerable adult has access to the criminal justice system. Otherwise, practice that results in only 'welfare'-based responses to adult abuse decriminalises acts that in any other walk of life would be deemed a criminal offence (Williams, 2000) and serves to justify oppressive and discriminatory responses on the part of organisations and practitioners. (Galpin and Parker, 2007)*

Practice analysis

The Mental Capacity Act 2005

In much the same way that the approach to risk is evolving at a structural level, there has also been a significant shift in the way the issue of mental capacity is being viewed. The implementation of the Mental Capacity Act 2005 has been described as a 'significant landmark' in the law relating to vulnerable adults (Johns, 2007). It attempts to balance an individual's rights with the desire to protect them and provides a more comprehensive legal framework for decision-making on behalf of those vulnerable adults who have lost capacity. This legislation takes a less oppressive approach through the recognition that capacity is decision specific and individuals have the right to make decisions even if these are deemed to be 'unwise' by others.

The elements of empowerment and protection within the Mental Capacity Act 2005 are demonstrated in the case of Mrs Ensor. When she was assessed prior to October 2007 as lacking the ability to make decisions, this applied to all areas of her life. Recently, when considering discharge from the Intermediate Care Unit, the social worker only assessed whether she was able to decide where she wanted to live. One would presume she had capacity to make decisions in other areas, unless proved otherwise.

To assess mental capacity, the social worker is required to take Mrs Ensor's past and present wishes and feelings, beliefs and values into account along with considering the views of her daughter and husband when making the 'best interest' decision. Mrs Ensor has the right to privacy and family life under the Human Rights Act 1998 and for her this meant a return home where the risks were managed with a care package rather than a residential admission. As a result of the ongoing conflict between Mr Ensor and his daughter, and the danger of Mrs Ensor's wishes becoming lost, an Independent Mental Capacity Advocate (IMCA) could be considered in order to ensure that her wishes and feelings continue to be taken into account.

The Mental Capacity Act 2005 establishes five principles that should be followed when working within the framework of the Act. These principles support practice where issues of mental capacity may be an issue.

- A person must be assumed to have capacity unless it is established that he lacks capacity.

- A person is not to be treated as unable to make a decision unless all practicable steps to help him to do so have been taken without success.

- A person is not to be treated as unable to make a decision merely because he makes an unwise decision.

- An act done, or decision made, under this Act for or on behalf of a person who lacks capacity must be done, or made, in his best interests.

- Before the act is done, or the decision made, regard must be had to whether the purpose for which it is needed can be as effectively achieved in a way that is less restrictive of the person's rights and freedom of action.

(Brown and Barber, 2008, p5–6)

The Mental Capacity Act 2005 and the Deprivation of Liberty Safeguards

The Deprivation of Liberty Safeguards (DOLS) are an integral part of the Mental Capacity Act 2005.

- The DOLS Safeguards protect people who lack the capacity to consent to the arrangements made for their own safety, in either hospitals or care homes.

- They protect against the arbitrary detention of people who lack the capacity to consent to the arrangements made for their care or treatment and who need to be deprived of their liberty, in their own best interests.

- They rectify the breach of Article 5 of the European Convention on Human Rights identified by the European Court of Human Rights in HL v UK 2004 (the 'Bournewood' case).

- In HL v UK the European Court of Human Rights found breaches of Articles 5(1) and 5(4):

  o 'Everyone has the right to liberty and security of person. No one shall be deprived of his liberty save in the following cases, and in accordance with a procedure prescribed by law . . .'

  o 'Everyone who is deprived of his liberty shall be entitled to take proceedings by which the lawfulness of his detention shall be decided speedily by a court, and released if the detention is not lawful'.

More recent cases have appeared that support practitioners in making decisions in the context of DOLS; for example, JE v DE(1), Surrey CC (2), 2006.

ACTIVITY **2.5**

What case law do you use to support your decision-making?

Practitioner reflections

As a social work practitioner I feel that the Mental Capacity Act (2005) in addition to providing safeguards to service users has also been beneficial for social workers and provided much needed clarification in this area. One of the areas that I find most challenging as a practitioner is working with individuals to assert their rights and promote independence while also protecting them and others from harm (GSCC, 2002).

The point at which to operate on a 'care or control' continuum is usually defined by the service user's mental capacity (Clark, 1998). Prior to the introduction of the Mental Capacity Act 2005, social workers would often encounter individuals who had not had a formal assessment or were deemed to have capacity, yet the worker had doubts or concerns about whether they had insight or fully understood the decision that had to be made. The new law greatly reduces these 'grey' areas and provides a clear framework for documenting and recording professional decision-making.

Anti-oppressive practice

Thompson (2003) suggests oppression and discrimination are interrelated,
nation giving rise to oppression.

- *Is this your experience in practice?*

- *What impact has this had on your service users and/or carers?*

- *How do you ensure your practice is anti-oppressive and anti-discriminatory?*

Discussion of the above areas highlights how social workers need to have an understanding of a wide range of issues which impact upon the lives of older adults if they are to practise in an anti-oppressive and anti-discriminatory manner. It has been demonstrated that this needs to go beyond the personal level and include cultural and structural factors. While this may seem a considerable challenge, one way in which it can begin to be achieved is through taking a life-course approach to ageing. This model builds on Erikson's life cycle model (1963, 1982, cited in Stuart-Hamilton, 2000, p145), although it has been argued his work reinforces socially expected Euro-centric notions of 'normal' life stage development. However, it does provide a useful framework on which to develop a life-course approach. This is non-prescriptive and views ageing in relation to the life-course as a whole rather than a separate entity, and explores the past, current situation and aspirations for the future (Tanner and Harris, 2008). This is an ideal model for taking into account the areas discussed in this chapter. The notion that an individual's past experiences shape the person they are today allows factors at a personal, cultural and structural level to be considered and issues around discrimination, inequality and oppression to be acknowledged.

A life-course approach is very person-centred, provides a holistic assessment and view of the person, and incorporates key social work values. Research has found that taking a biographical or narrative approach, both of which incorporate life-course principles, brings positive results. These include a greater appreciation of issues around diversity and oppression, generation of trust between the older person and the professional, and reduced power imbalances (Gearing and Coleman, 1996 cited in Tanner and Harris, 2008, p141; Richards, 2000; Milner and O'Byrne, 2002). It can also influence decisions about appropriate service provision (Richards, 2002).

Practitioner reflections

On a personal level, I have found that a life-course approach provides a greater understanding of the individual, what is important to them and what interventions they are likely to find acceptable. It also enables the older person's 'voice' and story to be heard, the importance of which should not be underestimated.

Chapter summary

- Practitioners working with older people need to be aware of the role of ageism and the impact of cultural beliefs on risk assessment and management, in particular older people's self-perception and the views held by relatives and professionals.

- The National Service Framework (NSF) (DH, 2001a) provides a good foundation for social work practice with older people, aiming to eliminate age discrimination and provide person-centred care.

- Knowledge of the law is extremely important in practice, but frequently it is marginalised by other factors, such as internal policies and procedures. While these remain important, the law is integral to social work practice and provides a foundation on which to build good practice with vulnerable adults.

- The Mental Capacity Act 2005 advocates both empowerment and protection for vulnerable individuals and has had a significant effect on social work practice with older adults.

- The meaning of dependency is narrowly defined in practice and often related to policy. However, practitioners need to look beyond policy to the individual to understand the relationships and needs of older people.

- A life-course approach to ageing is person-centred and incorporates key social work values. It provides a holistic assessment and view of the person, acknowledging what is important to individuals and what service provision is most appropriate for them.

Chapter 3

The rising profile of informal care: modernisation and the future of carers' services

Sally Lee

ACHIEVING A POST-QUALIFYING SPECIALIST AWARD IN SOCIAL WORK WITH ADULTS

This chapter demonstrates how you might meet the GSCC specialist standards and requirements for post-qualifying social work education and training.

Legislation, social policy and social welfare

Social workers will need to extend and apply their knowledge and understanding of all relevant legal frameworks, social policies and social welfare principles within their particular area of practice. This includes all relevant legal and policy frameworks and the range of statutory responsibilities associated with working with adults. It also includes relevant legal and policy frameworks relating to mental health and the welfare of children and young people, together with the law relating to equality legislation and human rights.

Inter-professional, multi-agency working, networking, community-based services and accountability

In order to contribute to an integrated and comprehensive assessment and care plan, social workers need to know how to work with other professionals and other teams and services. This includes engaging with mental health, children and young people's services as well as health, education, criminal justice, probation, employment, leisure and housing services. They also need to know how to work with service user and carer-led organisations, and other community-based facilities and resources.

Introduction

Informal carers form the backbone of the British care system. Three in five of us will be informal carers at some point in our lives – 58 per cent women, 42 per cent men (Carers

UK, 2009) – and there were approximately 1.5 million adult social care workers in Britain during 2007/08 (CSCI, 2009). At any one time six million people in the UK are providing support valued at £87 billion (Carers UK, 2008). Yet informal carers, as a valuable and valued asset, have only recently been fully acknowledged in community care legislation and social policy.

This chapter will examine why this is and evaluate whether acknowledgement in law and social policy will improve the lives of carers. Analysis of the application of carers' policy at a local and national level will be developed and consideration given to future service provision in light of the modernisation of social care, which is currently introducing new ways of working with service users and carers and supports a change in role for both informal carers and social work professionals.

Facts about caring (www.carersuk.org)

'Carers UK: the voice of carers' provides information on the nature and extent of carers in the UK today. It suggests that:

- *one in eight adults are carers (approximately six million people);*
- *everyday another 6,000 people take on a caring responsibility;*
- *carers save the economy £87 billion per year, an average of £15,260 per carer;*
- *over three million people juggle care with work, with one in five carers giving up work altogether;*
- *the main carer's benefit is £53.10 for a minimum of 35 hours per week, equivalent of £1.52 per hour (this is far below the national minimum wage of £5.73 per hour);*
- *carers providing high levels of care are twice as likely to be permanently sick or disabled;*
- *625,000 suffer mental and physical ill health as a direct consequence of the demands of caring;*
- *1.25 million people provide over 50 hours of care per week.*

Carers UK has called upon the government to improve conditions for carers, suggesting the carers' benefit system must:

- *protect carers from falling into poverty;*
- *reflect carers' different circumstances;*
- *help carers combine caring with paid work and study;*
- *be easy to access and make a claim.*

Why care?

When considering care in the social care domain, be it unpaid, informal, formal or professional, one question leaps to mind: why do we bother? This is an important question because its answer provides some insight into the motivation of carers and enables government to develop policy and legislation to support practice with carers. To understand why individuals care, we first need to define what care is. There are various definitions of care; however, in the context of this chapter, a definition developed by Fisher and Tronto (1990) is used. They define care as:

> *[A] species of activity that includes everything we do to maintain, continue and repair our 'world' so that we can live in it as well as possible. That world includes our bodies, ourselves, and our environment, all of which we seek to interweave in a complex, life sustaining web (cited in Sevenhuijsen, 2000, p3).*

This is a useful definition because it is global, encompassing the practical, concrete, hands-on care provided by carers on a daily basis and alludes to a wider ethical or moral code by which individuals live their lives. Therefore one could argue that 'care should be seen as both an activity and a disposition' (Tronto, 1993, p118 in Sevenhuijsen, 2000, p14). While a distinction can be drawn between informal carers who provide care within a relationship and the care demonstrated by social workers, the underlying motivation is drawn from the same source – to maintain our 'world'. This definition also acknowledges that care-giving satisfies instinctual human self-interest, for although care is something given, in so doing we make our world better for ourselves.

A utilitarian argument would acknowledge the mutual personal benefits to individuals which care provides, but would require a rational calculation of the costs as well as benefits. At the point where the cost becomes greater, the carer would give up. However, it might be argued humans are not so rational and this ignores the complex 'ties which bind' (Twigg and Atkin, 2002) that make informal carers continue despite the personal cost, and social care workers continue to seek to improve lives and address inequalities despite the continuation of social problems such as poverty. Twigg and Atkin (2002) argue that because of this irrationality, 'carers' pose moral responsibilities to welfare agencies precisely because they cannot be assumed to pursue their interests in a straightforward way (p10). How such moral responsibilities are met has arguably depended on how others, such as feminist and political ideological foundations of successive governments, have interpreted the role of carers within care provision.

Understanding ideology

- *Ideology is a set of ideas which are associated with a particular set of social arrangements. Ideology has the effect of legitimatising the status quo (Thompson, 2001).*

- *In the context of social work, ideology refers to the ideas, beliefs and assumptions that reflect power relations within society and which impact on policy and practice with adults.*

- *Ideology provides the link between the objective world of social circumstances and the internal subjective world of meaning. Ideology has the ability to become so ingrained that its validity is unquestioned, it becomes the 'taken-for-grantedness of everyday life' (Thompson, 2003).*

- *A consequence of ideology is that it perpetuates assumptions we make about individuals, or groups of individuals, and influences our actions and reactions to them.*

- *Billig (2001) suggests through ideology the inequalities of society will appear as 'natural' or 'inevitable'. For example patriarchy made it appear 'natural' that women were not considered full citizens and denied the vote, while undertaking a caring role is 'inevitable' for women.*

Feminism and the ethics of care

ACTIVITY 3.2

- *Does gender make a difference to society's expectations of who should provide care?*

- *Do you think females are put under more pressure to undertake a caring role? If so, why?*

- *Does gender influence your practice with carers in any way?*

There is an ongoing debate concerning the ethics of care, a branch of philosophical ethics developed by feminists such as Carol Gilligan and Ned Noddings (Meagher and Parton, 2004) in the 1970s and 1980s. This approach emphasises the 'Interdependence of humans and their responsibilities to each other, recognises the moral worth of all persons, emphasises caring as a moral posture or disposition [with] each moral decision taking place in a specific context [and] that caring is a process that fosters growth of those in a caring relationship' (Meagher and Parton, 2004, p15). This links to the earlier definition of care in terms of the interdependence of the world and indicates that care is fundamentally a 'good' thing: good for the individuals concerned and good for the wider community.

The ethics of care was developed in response to rights-based ethics which sought to supersede relational attachments. Feminists developed the concept of 'care focused feminism', which 'regards women's capacity for care as a human strength which can and should be taught to men as well as women' (Sevenhuijensen, 2000, p16). Tronto (1993) broadened the concept of the ethics of care from the interpersonal to include the political. Tronto suggested care is a political as well as a moral concept, emphasising the importance of equality and justice, recognising the issues of power concerned with care both on a macro level where 'class, gender and race interact to distribute both the getting and giving of care' (cited Meagher and Parton, 2004, p17) and the micro level where care givers potentially have more power (Meagher and Parton, 2004). Therefore, the political context plays an important role in defining the role and purpose of carers at a personal level in society. Within this political context, ideology is key to shaping both service development and social work practice in supporting carers.

Carers in a political context

ACTIVITY 3.3

From a political perspective, what factors have influenced the government's development of policy and legislation to support practice with carers?

Carers were an unacknowledged group in social care legislation and policy until the 1990s (NHS Community Care Act 1990), which saw the re-emergence of neo-liberalism under the Conservative governments of the 1980s and 1990s. Neo-liberal ideology places great emphasis on the role of the individual, rationality (characterised by the pursuit of self-interest) and the supremacy of the markets in the development and delivery of social care. This led to the government introducing principals of the free market into social care where clients are considered consumers and social workers care managers and gatekeepers. From this perspective care is viewed as a commodity that is no longer associated with altruism or love alone, but is part of regulated services in social care provision (Orme, 2002).

This view diverged from the preceding post-war policy of welfare capitalism based on Keynesian collectivist values, which sought to ensure that all citizens have the resources needed to participate in the social (and economic) life of society (Brown, 2006). The Beveridge Report (1942), the basis for post-war welfare reform, sought to 'vanquish the "five giant evils" of "want, ignorance, squalor, disease and idleness"' (Beveridge, cited Beresford, 2005, p466). The state was seen as having responsibility for 'managing the economy in a way that reduces instability, minimises unemployment and eliminates poverty' (Brown, 2006, p2) and was seen as a way of creating social justice through the distribution of resources via universal national insurance. Economic growth would be used to fund welfare to support the old, disabled and unemployed and to supply services such as education, health and social services to all (Brown, 2006). This reflected the prevailing view of society at that time concerning the ideological triangle of nation, family and work which conceived the 'normal' family – British, white, able bodied – as the cornerstone of society. The division of labour was on gender lines with women generally being the nurturers and carers who did not need acknowledgement, assistance or protection in law because they were doing what 'came naturally' (author's emphasis).

However, these assumptions were questioned in the 1970s and 1980s as a feminist critique of community care sought to challenge the implicit assumption in social policy: first, that women were the carers; and second, 'Women were seen as the new reserve army of – this time – unpaid labour' (Twigg and Atkin, 2002, p3). This challenge was based on 'feminist debates concerning childcare, the role of women's unpaid labour and the significance of the family in public policy' (Twigg and Atkin, 2002, p3).

While this debate, and the feminist movement, was evolving and influencing the development of social policy and legislation (e.g., the Sex Discrimination Act 1975), the disability movement (e.g., Carers UK which began in 1965 and Age Concern which took over from the National Old People's Welfare Committee) was gaining momentum and influence. Furthermore, the economic growth upon which welfare capitalism relied was severely affected by world recession in the 1970s. Beresford (2005) suggests 'poverty continued to be a problem . . . in addition by its very nature and underpinning values and assumptions, the welfare state frequently reinforced rather than challenged inequalities and exclusions on the basis of gender, class, ethnicity, disability, age and sexuality' (p487). The world itself was changing with the rise of globalisation, which rested 'on low and stable inflation, low levels of taxation, low wages and flexible labour markets in order not to frighten off globally mobile investment and to compete on equal terms in a global economy' (Beresford, 2005, p473).

The conditions to support change from post-war notions of the welfare state to a neo-liberal approach was confirmed with the election of the New Right under the leadership of Margaret Thatcher, and in other Anglo-Saxon states, such as the USA and Australia, of governments which promoted the principles of 'global economic forces' and imposed 'new regimes of market austerity on their public services, and economic competition on their citizens' (Jordan, 2000, p3). Neo-liberalism argues against state welfare intervention, seeing it as 'costly, wasteful, bureaucratic, centralising and inefficient' (Beresford, 2005, p478). State welfare was viewed as creating dependence, undermining the market and curbing individual choice and freedom.

Neo-liberal ideology suggests that individuals are responsible for their situation and the state should provide only a safety net and a framework of law within which individuals operate and are protected from each other. This is based on the notion of individuals as holders of rights, and Meagher and Parton (2004) point out that such political systems do not trust the moral capacity of its citizens but rely on the law to guarantee morality. This approach to welfare provision favours a mixed economy of care where responsibility for provision lies first with the individual, then their family, followed by community support networks and the voluntary sector with the state being the last resort. In this context, the free market is seen as responsive to individual preferences and efficient because the free market is able to respond to need speedily as demand stimulates provision, unlike government.

However, Beresford argues that the New Right's switch in policy from welfare capitalism was made with no evidence 'to demonstrate either the inferiority of state welfare provision [in relation to market provision] or the superiority of market welfare provision [in relation to state provision]' (Pierson, 1991 cited in Beresford, 2005, p470). Rather than being evidence-based, this shift in perspective reflected changing government ideology that supported a reduction in the development and delivery of state welfare, suggesting the state instead of addressing social ills had actually created them, while also being inefficient and expensive.

It is interesting then, in light of the neo-liberal desire to 'roll back the state', that carers' first acknowledgment in legislation and policy came during the Conservative era. The White Paper *Caring for People*, which led to the NHS and Community Care Act 1990, stated that one of the key objectives is 'to ensure that service providers make practical support for carers a high priority' (DH, 1989, Para 1.11). However, the New Right 'was not explicitly engaged with the issue of informal care, though the subject is present obliquely in the emphasis on personal responsibility for welfare and the promotion of conservative family values' (Twigg and Atkin, 2002, p5). This legislative acknowledgement of carers reflected government's fiscal concerns in supporting carers as this was seen as more cost effective than the state providing direct services, which it suggested harbours dependency and undermines the market (Twigg and Atkin, 2005).

The first piece of legislation specifically concerning carers came with the Carers (Recognition and Services) Act 1995. This Act entitled carers who provided regular and substantial care to request an assessment if the cared-for person had been assessed under the NHS and Community Care Act 1990. Local authorities were obliged to take the carer's ability to sustain care into account when devising care packages for individuals (Carers UK, 2009). Practice would now require that an assessment of an individual take account of the sustainability of their care network. This Act gave carers important new rights and a clearer legal status. However, the Act did not provide for standardised services across local authorities, which arguably led to variable service provision – the notion of the 'postcode lottery' which carers have campaigned against (Carers UK, 2008). The power to enable services to be provided for carers came with the implementation of the Carers and Disabled Children Act 2000 after the Labour party returned to power in 1997. This provided local authorities with the power to offer services specifically to carers, including direct payments.

The 1999 Carer's Strategy, *Caring about Carers* (DH, 1999a), provides further guidance on the direction of travel for carers' services. Tony Blair wrote in the foreword to the strategy that informal carers are the best example of what he meant by strong communities and people having responsibility for each other, stating 'Caring is personal. It is individual. But it is social too: and the government can help in its own way.' This strategy, and subsequent legislation, sought to provide carers with better information, support and rights to have their own health needs met. Blair stated 'Caring for carers is a vital element in caring for those who need care' (1999a, p2).

The Blair government, under the banner of 'New Labour', did not return to the old-style welfare capitalism of previous Labour governments, but rather introduced the politics of the Third Way to Britain. Jordan (2000) argues that the Third Way 'attempts to combine elements of individualism with aspects of collectivism' (p42) – a bringing together of the best of Beveridge and the New Right – by delivering Labour values through neo-liberal economic policy. These values include: 'equality (in terms of individual moral worth, opportunity, protection); autonomy (freedom, choice, liberty); community (rights and responsibilities, obligations, social inclusion) and democracy (devolution, empowerment)'

(Jordan, 2000, p20). The emphasis by successive Labour governments since 1997 has been on social inclusion, especially through participation in work and education as not only do they engender economic opportunity but they also encourage self-esteem, purpose and responsibility. The government sees the state as having a responsibility to support individuals in need of assistance to enable them to attain citizenship rights, but in attaining such rights individuals have a responsibility to their community (local and national) not to live at the expense of others. As a matter of justice, the state should clearly define and, where necessary, enforce the obligations which derive from these basic responsibilities (Brown, 2006). Arguably, in this political context, obligation in care provision is related to the definition of 'care' offered earlier; it is about maintaining our world and being interdependent in a more global sense.

The 1999 Carer's Strategy led to the Carers (Equal Opportunities) Act 2004, which introduced assistance for carers who wish to work or access education, training or leisure. Clements (2007) suggests this Act mirrored a shift in perspective on the role of carers from unpaid providers to people in their own right where, instead of focusing on sustaining the caring role as in previous legislation, the target of the 2004 Act was to promote inclusion through work/training/leisure. However, research by CSCI in their 2006 report State of Social Care in England found that the increased emphasis on carers at the strategic level had not been translated into action on the ground as 'carer's responsibilities are increased by the trend towards ever tighter eligibility criteria for access to services' (Clements, 2007, p11). Thus a gap appears to have developed between the intention of policy and its implementation at a local level.

Practice experience suggests some local authorities have developed their own local carers' strategies, which emphasise greater co-working between the council and other agencies in order to better identify carers and provide information and services, such as short breaks and opportunities for work and training. Consultation with carers' groups has indicated that carers are unsure of where to get support and they report having mixed experiences of assessments. Many have said they have not been offered assessments and those who have say frequently nothing happens (Carers UK, 2008).

Carers and personalisation: *The Pro–Am Revolution*

As policy and legislation has developed to support carers, so has the government's view of the role of the professional and carer in social care provision. *The Pro–Am Revolution* (Leadbeater and Miller, 2004) outlines how personalisation facilitates the process of reducing demarcation between professionals and non-professionals, seen as a key principle by government in restructuring public services (National School of Government, 2007). This report asserts that, during the twentieth century, activities that had once been in the realm of the amateur were professionalised as they became more organised and 'knowledge and procedures were codified and regulated' (p12). For example, voluntary organisations coordinated and provided care for the deserving poor; however, these roles were eventually taken over by social workers and professional carers. This resulted in professionals becoming more valued and the amateur less. However, Leadbeater and Miller

(2004) argue that in the last 20 years these roles have changed and the amateur now operates at a professional level as a professional amateur, or Pro–Am. The report goes on to highlight the areas in which Pro–Ams have been successful; for example in astronomy, software development and online games. They argue professionals need to accept they can no longer control knowledge from their 'ivory' towers (p16) and need to work with Pro–Ams to resolve problems, as the relationship between professionals and amateurs becomes more fluid (p23).

The authors suggest this route should not be left just to areas such as astronomy, but also 'the path that our health, education, and welfare systems follow' (p16). In this context, carers are seen as equal partners to professional carers. While apparent equality brings with it rights, it also requires carers to engage in additional responsibilities; for example, in managing a direct payment.

Therefore, the roles of both the professional and the carer are evolving.

The changing role of the social work professional

ACTIVITY 3.4

- *In your professional experience, how has policy and legislation impacted on your practice with carers?*

- *In your personal experience, how has policy and legislation impacted on your role as a carer; for example, as a parent or child?*

Social care policy is currently undergoing a radical overhaul through the Transforming Social Care agenda outlined in *Putting People First* (DH, 2007b). This has been prompted by increasing demand on services as a result of an aging population, with the media suggesting the number of individuals aged 85 years plus in the UK will double by 2018 (Benjamin, 2008) bringing with it an increase in the number of carers to 13 million (Carers UK, 2008). This agenda builds on and is a continuation of the modernisation programme set out in the 1998 White Paper *Modernising Social Services* (DH, 1998a). This White Paper suggested that change in social services was required because of low public confidence and the poor quality of many services in terms of protection of the vulnerable, along with poor coordination between agencies, inflexibility of services, lack of clarity of role and standards, inconsistencies across the country in provision, and cost characterised by inefficiency. Jordan (2000) argues that local authority social work grew in the 1980s and 1990s as the focus of practice moved from care to 'greater emphasis on social control, and a policy shift from social justice to criminal justice' (p17). The government has continued this trend with an emphasis on regulating local authorities through new standards and targets to measure performance and the creation of new agencies to enforce these, as part of the 'relentless drive for greater accountability' (Jordan, 2000. p9).

The third sector, or not for profit agencies, rather than local authorities have been given an increasing role in service provision for carers. They undertake traditional social work

roles leaving state social workers to tasks of surveillance and control through the collection of data required to meet performance indicators. This leads to a position where 'the provision of such data, alongside keeping in budget have become the twin imperatives against which social workers' performance is measured and monitored' (Jones, cited in Ferguson et al., 2005, p104).

The role of state social work appears to be narrowing as the Green Paper, *Independence Well-being and Choice* (DH, 2005) and the White Paper, *Our Health, Our Care, Our Say* (DH, 2006) have developed the theme of personalisation. The Health and Social Care Act 2008 has increased access to direct payments to include those previously excluded by expanding the potential of direct payments via 'indirect' direct payments to carers for those who may lack mental capacity, whereby increasing carer power and control as well as responsibility.

The introduction of individualised budgets will bring together funding from different streams, such as social care, community equipment, ILF and DFG (Carr and Robbins, 2009) and again change the professional role. Social work activity is now defined in terms of brokerage, advocacy or navigators who support individuals to design and manage their care while they monitor spending of monies. Research indicates that the bureaucratisation of social work through care management, FACS, performance indicators and the awareness of 'the budget' and a generalised culture of blame makes social workers 'institutionally captured by the dominant bureaucratic/rationing regime' (Hudson, 2009).

Ruth Cartwright, a BASW professional officer for England, warns against the devaluing of social workers, stating 'while Local Authorities will continue to need social workers under personalisation for safeguarding and complex cases, other work is being transferred to cheaper non-qualified staff' and she knows of two councils now planning to significantly reduce adult care social work staff' (2009, p5). With the announcement of public services budget cuts of £15 billion in the 2009/10 budget (BBC Radio 4, *Today Programme*, 2009), more councils are likely to do the same. A social work taskforce has recently been formed to work with government on the review of adult services; BASW report that this may be the last chance to save adult social work (Community Care, 2009, p5).

One question we might consider is: If the social work profession does decrease in numbers and/or sees a significant change in its role, what might this mean for carers?

The changing role of informal carers

ACTIVITY 3.5

Team discussion

- *What is your expectation of the role carers will play in service provision in adult social care in the future?*

- *How do the carers you currently support view their future as carers?*

- *How does government, at a national and local level, view the role of carers in the future?*

Ask each team member to write a list of the similarities and differences in responses and discuss how you might use your findings to improve practice with carers in your team.

Our Health Our Care, Our Say (DH, 2006) identified more support for carers as a specific goal. The government announced in its 'New Deal for Carers' that by 2018 their aim is 'for carers to be respected as expert care partners with personalised services to support them in their caring role; have a life of their own alongside their caring role; financial support so they are not forced into hardship; support so they stay mentally and physically well and support for young carers so they do not undertake inappropriate care' (DH, 2006, p7).

Research summary: the health and well-being of young carers

- *The 2001 census data suggests 114,000 (1.4 per cent of all) children aged 5–15 were providing 'informal' care for family members;*

- *18,000 (6.3 per cent) provided 20 hours or more care per week;*

- *9,000 (3.1 per cent) provided 50 hours or more care per week;*

- *the average age of young carers was 12 years old;*

- *research also suggests more girls than boys act as young carers;*

- *children are more likely to become young carers for an ill or disabled parent if their family lacks sufficient personal or financial support.*

Research findings are equivocal on the long term effects on young people of caring. Being a young carer, especially where personal and practical support is lacking, can affect elements of the child's transition to adulthood. The educational and employment opportunities of young carers may also be adversely affected. (SCIE, 2005)

To increase support for all carers, the government launched a national information helpline and website, a training programme for carers to inform carers of their rights, and an additional £25 million for emergency respite. A review of the 1999 Carer's Strategy led to the publication of *Carers at the Heart of 21st Century Families and Communities* (DH, 2008b). This document emphasised the importance of carers now and in the future. Ivan Lewis, Social Care Minister, stated that because of the aging population in the next decade, 'elder care will be the new childcare, and it is essential our policies properly meet the scale of the challenge' (Benjamin, 2008, p3).

The language of the updated carers' strategy is extremely pro-carers seeing them as 'fundamental to strong families and stable communities' (DH, 2008b, p7). It clarifies the government's view of the roles of carers and families – 'the strategy aims to support people and their carers in their own homes and communities wherever possible' (DH, 2008b, p13).

It also outlines its own responsibilities in terms of providing leadership, monitoring implementation, setting overall objectives and helping join up services. In addition, it highlights the responsibilities of wider society to value carers, and for employers to enable carers to work. It recognises the effects care can have on a carer's own health and plans to pilot annual health checks for carers. All of which appears well and good; however, carers need to be recognised as carers to be in receipt of the above services.

While CSCI (2009) identifies that there was a 25 per cent increase in the number of carers receiving a service and that the number of carers' breaks increased in 2007/08, issues persist around the low number of carers being offered assessments and subsequent services. Less than 400,000 assessments or reviews were undertaken in 2005/06 (Hunter, 2007), which appears minimal if one considers that there is estimated to be six million carers in Britain (Carers UK, 2008).

There is also a dilemma between the Personalisation Agenda and FACS that some suggest needs to be resolved. The latter is used as a rationing tool prescribing eligibility for services, whereas the former is concerned with self-assessment, choice and care designed to respond to individual need 'focused on a wide definition of health and wellbeing' (Henwood and Hudson, 2008). CSCI has alerted government to the contradiction between the FACS system and the aspirations of personalisation.

The implementation of the personalisation agenda is in the early stages so the advantages or not for carers is not yet clear. However, CSCI (2009) highlights concerns about how government is expecting the personalisation agenda to be applicable to all but 'not everyone is convinced that Individual Budgets will work well for people with multiple and complex needs' (p8). Carers are concerned that additional responsibilities for care will fall to them, which Clements (2008a) identifies as a real concern as the government is expecting personalisation to be cost neutral with the expectation that the individual and their support network are more involved in organising the care. He argues that the way the policy is written suggests that individuals who do not use their family or carers to help manage the package may be worse off, and are more likely to put pressure on their family/carer to become involved. Carers UK (2008) suggest that although 73 per cent of respondents thought direct payments as part of personalisation brought better services, only 57 per cent would recommend them and 37 per cent had mixed feelings because of the increased responsibilities direct payments bring in terms of recruitment and employment (Carers UK, 2008).

This suggests carers are not a homogenous group and services need to be flexible to reflect these differences. There is an approximate turnover of two million informal carers each year (Carers UK, 2008). This necessitates the availability of high-quality information for those starting out to ensure they are aware of their rights, and for those ceasing, specialist assistance to support them getting back into the workplace or to deal with the practical and emotional loss of their caring role. The national information line detailed in the strategy may help to provide this.

In addition, carers have expressed their wish to be seen as equal partners by social care workers and the strategy states the aim of carers being viewed as expert care partners. For this to be achieved, acknowledgement about power differentials is necessary. The language of government policy is one of equality and partnership between carers and agencies, defining the responsibilities of the state, families and the third sector. But this has to be translated into action on the ground for it to have credibility, which means that carers again need to be informed of their rights and social care workers need to have up-to-date information about local services and entitlements.

For example, Carers UK (2008) has called on the government to radically overhaul the benefit and tax systems in order to address carer poverty, and Imelda Redmond, Chief

Executive of Carers UK, argues that carers themselves will be very angry that there is no recognition by government (in the strategy) of the poverty in which many of them are living (Benjamin, 2008). Gordon Brown has suggested that as part of the review currently being undertaken into the funding of adult care services, we must also find the right approach to ensuring a fairer deal for our carers that provides financial support, particularly to those who face hardship (DH, 2008a). However, this will not be completed until 2018, which is not soon enough for those carers facing hardship.

Successive governments since the 1980s have acknowledged the significance of carers, and the current administration is implementing policies in response to carers' needs as represented by organisations such as Carers UK and the Princess Royal Trust for Carers. Shan Nicholas, Chief Executive of the Princess Royal Trust for Carers, suggests they have put carers on the map (Hunter, 2007). However, it could be argued that the government's concern for carers goes beyond those raised by carers' organisations. A combination of collectivist and individualistic ideology in Third Way policy has meant that an obligation towards, and caring for, each other and our communities is recognised as a key factor in achieving a cohesive society which therefore makes care worthy of government support.

While a focus on carers is welcomed, one might also consider if increasing support for carers brings with it increasing expectations by government, which is consistent with the Third Way mantra of 'rights and responsibilities'. Government appears committed to developing entitlements to support the caring role, be that financial, emotional or psychological; however, it also requires carers to continue with their caring responsibilities.

Government appears to view carers as resources, service users and co-workers whom they also want to support to ensure they have the opportunity to engage in paid employment, leisure and educational activities.

Linking policy, legislation and practice: the relationship between the politics of care and the personal experiences of carers

Professional and political perceptions of carers

Sharkey (2000) identifies four models of carers as perceived by health and social care professionals, suggesting where professionals locate carers within the four models might have some impact on their practice. The four models are as follows.

Carers as resources

In this model, the agency regards carers as a resource. The agency's primary focus is on the cared for person. The carer is a vital resource but not the agency's primary concern. Concern for the carer in this model is limited.

> ### Carers as co-workers
>
> *In this model the agency see themselves as working in tandem with the carer, or 'inter-weaving'. Interweaving is the notion that the formal service and informal sector co-operate in a spirit of partnership and trust.*
>
> ### Carers as co-service users
>
> *The carer is viewed as a service user, as someone in need of help in their own right due possibly to their own frailty or due to carer stress. Possible conflicts between the carer and service user's needs are fully recognised.*
>
> ### The superseded carer
>
> *The carer is viewed as an individual and the aim of support is to enable the carer to transcend the care-giving relationship. In this model, the professional identifies the carer's desire to maximise their independence and supports the carer to be freed from their caring role/responsibilities.*
>
> *(Sharkey, 2000, p23)*

Twigg and Atkin (2002, pp12–15) offer a useful analysis of the four models, highlighting how they define the relationship between the state and carer and suggesting that, at the time of writing, policy did not identify what support for carers would be or for whom, so how carers were seen to fit into service provision remained ambiguous. This was, and continues to be, a challenge for practitioners and service providers. Their analysis suggests the first model, carers as resources, is an attractive approach for cash-strapped authorities and has been the prevailing view of governments and service providers where policy has focused on the maintaining of the caring relationship to affect cost savings in the provision of care.

The second model, they suggest, appeared to be a model that social care workers aspired to, and more recent findings suggest that carers want (Carers UK, 2009), with its suggestion of equality and cooperation. Yet anecdotal evidence would suggest in practice this may be problematic because of potential conflicts of interest. The view of 'carers as co-service users' appears to have been recognised by government as policy and legislation has given power to local authorities to assess carers separately and provide services directly to them. It would appear the last model has been especially favoured by the Labour government with its emphasis on independence and choice, but this has to be seen alongside their emphasis on family and community responsibility for each other, which utilises the carer as a resource. The Carers and Disabled Children's Act (2000) is focused on providing services to sustain, not supersede, the carer's role. For example, section 2.2 states:

> *The services referred to are any services which –*
>
> *(a) The local authority sees fit to provide and:*
>
> *(b) Will in the local authority's view help the carer care for the person cared for.*

Many practitioners identify carers as moving between the models suggested above as they interact with service providers at an individual relational level allowing for movement and fluidity between models. Sometimes a carer may be a resource and on other occasions they may be a service user in their own right. This relates to Twigg and Atkins's (2002) analysis of carers' attitudes to their role where again a carer can fit one model at one time and a different one at another; for example, when a carer feels engulfed and 'caring becomes the centre of their life, and the identifying feature of their self-identity' (p122). This often corresponds to the degree of care provided by the carer, the dynamics of the relationship and the circumstances in which they became a carer; for example, whether they had a choice. At times the engulfed carer is invisible, hidden behind the needs of the cared. Practice guidance of the 2000 Act describes such carers in terms of experiencing an extensive loss of autonomy and this is a critical risk which the local authority must respond to (Clements, 2007) as they have a general duty of care under common law to ensure carers 'are not exposed to unreasonable harm' (Clements, 2007, p25).

Carers can also move into the model of co-worker under a 'balancing/boundary setting mode where carers have a greater sense of autonomy and an understanding of their value as carers' (Twigg and Atkin, 2002, p124). Carers operating within this mode are more accepting of professional intervention and can be, and wish to be, viewed as co-workers who are able to articulate their own needs. For some carers their relationship with the cared for is symbiotic, as carers gain from their role and do not wish to be relieved of their responsibilities, but are often happy to accept a service providing their role is not threatened. However, difficulties can arise as a result of the conflicts of interest between carer and cared for over issues such as risk and independence.

Fluidity within perceptions of carers by government, practitioners and providers is required to understand the lived experience of carers. This is important as it allows practitioners to undertake a genuine personalised approach to supporting carers. However, it remains to be seen if policy and legislation goes with the flow of carers or presents a rigid system of support that exacerbates, rather than alleviates, the situation for carers.

Chapter summary

- Informal carers form the backbone of the British care system. Three in five of us will be informal carers at some point in our lives – 58 per cent women, 42 per cent men (Carers UK, 2009) – and there were approximately 1.5 million adult social care workers in Britain during 2007/08 (CSCI, 2009). At any one time six million people in the UK are providing support valued at £87 billion (Carers UK, 2008).

- Ideology plays an important role in determining how carers are viewed within society and how policy and legislation are developed to support them in their caring role.

- The role of social workers is currently undergoing radical change as social work activity is now defined in terms of brokerage and advocacy, where carers are supported to take on additional responsibilities to reduce the demarcation between the professional and informal carer.

- While a focus on carers is welcomed, one might also consider if increasing support for carers brings with it increasing expectations by government, which is consistent with the Third Way mantra of 'rights and responsibilities'. Government appears committed to developing entitlements to support the caring role, be that financial, emotional or psychological; however, it also requires carers to continue with their caring responsibilities.

- Fluidity within perceptions of carers by government, practitioners and providers is required to understand the lived experience of carers. This is important as it allows practitioners to undertake a genuine personalised approach to supporting carers. However, it remains to be seen whether policy and legislation will adequately support carers.

FURTHER READING

Adams, R. (2002) *Social policy for social work.* Basingstoke: Palgrave.

Bisman, C. (2004) Social work values, the moral core of the profession. *British Journal of Social Work,* 34: 109–123.

Burton, M. (2008) Grounding constructions of carers: exploring the experiences of carers through a grounded approach. *British Journal of Social Work,* 38: 493–506.

Community Care (2009) *Expert guide to personalisation,* 18 February. Online: **www.community-care.co.uk/Articles/2009/07/13/109083/personalisation.html.**

Howard, M. (2001) *Paying the price: carers, poverty and social exclusion.* London: Child Poverty Action Group.

Social Care Information and Learning Services (SCILS) (2008) *Individual learning session: assessing the needs of carers.* Update, June. Online: **www.scils.co.uk/carers.**

Chapter 4

Assessment and practice in learning disability services

Jill Small

ACHIEVING A POST-QUALIFYING SPECIALIST AWARD IN SOCIAL WORK WITH ADULTS

This chapter demonstrates how you might meet the GSCC specialist standards and requirements for post-qualifying social work education and training.

Communication and engagement

Communication with adults, including listening, engaging, empathising, finding out, explaining, advising, sharing information and summarising. This must take into account the full range of communication methods which enable them to meaningfully participate in their own assessment and planning and delivery of services. This includes effective work with interpreters, translators and independent advocates as appropriate, and identification of barriers to effective communication, including impact on self, institutional and organisational barriers.

Assessment, independence, risk, vulnerability and protection

Application of assessment models and frameworks to the assessment of needs, taking into account additional or complex needs and mental capacity. This includes the formulation of care plans, appropriate care and support packages and contribution to joint and multi-agency assessments.

Identification and management of risk, together with the ability to intervene in situations to reduce risks to individuals, their carers, families and dependents – this includes capacity to identify the abuse of vulnerable adults and their dependent children by others and working to safeguard them.

Support for service users with both shorter and longer term needs, with the aim of enabling them to live safely and as independently as possible in the place and communities of their own choice. This includes utilising knowledge about available support within their communities and knowledge of assistive technologies.

Introduction

This chapter is presented in two parts. Part one considers assessment in the context of the personalisation, community care, needs, rights and risk. Part two focuses on the practice analysis of two case studies which are used to examine issues of independence, self-determination, oppression and discrimination to explore how stereotypical assumptions about individuals with a learning disability might lead to powerlessness and increased vulnerability. Gilbert (2006) suggests the experiences of individuals with a disability are often much more to do with society's attitudes than their original impairment. It could be argued that this is particularly so for individuals with a learning disability.

Policy guidance: Valuing People

The White Paper, Valuing People, *defines a learning disability as:*

> *A significantly reduced ability to understand new or complex information (impaired intelligence) with reduced ability to cope independently (impaired social functioning) which started before adulthood, with a lasting effect on development. (DH, 2001b, p14)*

The dominant view of what constitutes a learning disability has been developed within the medical profession and appears to combine a medical and functional model of disability with emphasis on intelligence quotient below 70 and diagnosis of a condition usually associated with learning disability. However, as Williams (2006) highlights, intelligence quotient is not very helpful in defining learning disability as it does not reflect the person as a whole, merely their cognitive functioning. Statistically, approximately 3 per cent of the population has an intelligence quotient below 70 and most of these people will never come to the attention of services for people with learning disabilities. In addition, some surveys (Williams, 2006) have found people with an intelligence quotient of over 70 requiring support. Therefore the vulnerability of individuals with a learning disability is more complex than having impaired cognitive functioning.

Policy guidance: Valuing People

The White Paper suggests that intelligence quota:

> *Is not in itself, a sufficient reason for deciding whether an individual should be provided with additional health and social care support. An assessment of social functioning and communication skills should also be taken into account when determining need. (DH, 2001b, p15)*

No Secrets: Guidance on Developing and Implementing Multi-Agency Policies and Procedures to Protect Vulnerable Adults from Abuse (DH, 2000) defines a vulnerable adult as a person who:

is or may be in need of community care services by reason of mental or other disability, age or illness; and who is or may be unable to take care of him or herself, or unable to protect him or herself against significant harm or exploitation. (section 2.3)

This links with the need for services, in terms of community care, with an emphasis on individual limitations which could lead to some groups of people being considered as automatically vulnerable. However, it does not take into account wider structural factors that influence vulnerability. The same can be said of individuals with a learning disability where a learning disability is usually identified by 'limitations', 'impairments' and 'deficits' (Rapley, 2004) which contribute to the reinforcement of negative stereotypes, leading to social exclusion.

Community care and adult protection

Mandelstam (2009, p38) makes clear that adult protection undertaken in local authorities rests in community care legislation, stating:

> *This accounts for the reference in the guidance to a vulnerable adult having to be a person who may be in need of community care services. It is a direct reference to the same condition in s.47 of the NHS and Community Care Act 1990, which is the legal trigger for community care assessment of a person's need.*

Community care and personalisation

Research briefing

Personalisation is outlined by government in Putting People First *(DH, 2007b), as a central tenet in the reform of adult social care. This document outlines concepts such as person-centred practice and individual budgets (IBs) as tools practitioners can use to develop personalised services. An IB combines resources from different funding streams to which an individual is assessed as entitled. The resource allocation system (RAS) provides a process to decide how much money a person should get in their IB. This enables the individual to know how much money is available to spend on their support. Thus a framework for practice is developing.*

However, there are concerns that the drive in central and local government to reform service delivery and provision via personalisation appears to obscure the legislative framework that still supports practice.

Clements (2008b) clarifies the relationship between 'personalisation' and the NHS and Community Care Act 1990.

Clements states initiatives as outlined in Putting People First *(2007b):*

> *Must operate within the law, and this means that, in so far as they engage a local authority community care obligation, it must ensure that:*
>
> - *The person is being assessed under s.47 of the NHS and Community Care Act 1990.*

However, Clements (2007, p7) suggests in the context of personalisation it would appear that some local authorities think adherence to the 1990 Act is 'somehow optional' (p7), stating that:

> *Somehow self assessment and a RAS can substitute for a Community Care Assessment . . . The simple answer, of course, is that it cannot – policy (speculative or otherwise) cannot negate a legal right.*

While the language of government policy and guidance speaks of modernisation, personalisation and transformation, the NHS and Community Care Act 1990 provides the legal foundation on which practice should be developed.

Contemporary practice in adult services is focused on personalisation; however, lessons learnt from care management, in terms of understanding need, rights, risk, assessment and care management processes, provide a useful, as well as legal, foundation on which practitioners can build. The 'personalisation agenda' is not unlike the introduction of community care, which was also heralded as a new, and transformational, approach to social work practice, which was going to deliver more responsive services, of a higher quality and that were cost effective, and therefore offers much in enabling practitioners to avoid any pitfalls made in the implementation of community care.

There appears to be no agreement among writers regarding the origins of the term 'community care'. Lewis and Glennerster (1996, p1) suggest that governments have been attempting to introduce 'something called community care ever since at least 1948' when the newly created National Health Service wanted to rid itself of the old workhouses which were still in existence. These 'embarrassing institutions' contained people who were in need of nursing care, were unable to look after themselves or had nowhere else to go. The development of smaller units sited in the community was recommended. Studies of institutional care such as that carried out by Goffman in 1961 and the reports of neglect and abuse occurring in hospital settings strengthened the argument against hospital care for vulnerable people.

For people with learning disabilities, the publication of the White Paper *Better Services for the Mentally Handicapped* in 1971 was a landmark piece of social policy. One of its main recommendations was the replacement of 27,000 of 52,100 hospital places in England and Wales with residential homes in the community (Stevens, 2004). In the 1970s and

1980s, Thomas and Woods (2003) suggest 'normalisation' was of great influence in informing practice with people with learning disabilities. Normalisation proposes the provision of services to assist people with learning disabilities to have similar lifestyles to others and socially valued roles. This approach was influential in the development of practice in the context of community care services.

Means et al. (2003, p3) suggest the term 'community care' has changed over time and has been used by different governments to argue for 'changes in service emphasis'. One of these changes was the shift in the 1980s from care *in* the community to care *by* the community, with the role of the local authority to support informal care but not to replace it. The Griffith's report (1988) recommended a more coordinated approach to the management and funding of care which, along with assessment of need, was made the responsibility of the local authority. This was followed by the White Paper *Caring for People* (DH, 1989), which defined community care as 'providing the right level of intervention and support to enable people to achieve maximum independence and control over their own lives' (Means et al., 2003, p6). It introduced assessment and care management as the 'cornerstone' of high-quality care.

McDonald (2001) suggests that working in community care services requires the application of sound professional values because, in contrast to children's services, there is no unifying legislation when working with adults. McDonald explains that the National Health Service and Community Care Act 1990 did not replace existing legislation and has been 'added to piece meal' since 1990 with other legislation, such as that relating to carers, direct payments and disability discrimination. She also identifies that there was no explicit reference to racial and cultural needs in the 1990 legislation. In its 'comprehensive guide to assessment', the practice guidance (Department of Health and Social Services Inspectorate, 1991) makes very brief mention of the need to be aware of diversity but no specific instruction to consider these needs when undertaking assessments. The practitioner has been required to work with a wide range of policy and legislation with no clearly defined, or unifying, value base.

Need

ACTIVITY *4.1*

- *How would you define 'need'?*
- *What is this definition based on?*

The assessment of need has been central to social work practice under community care legislation. The National Health Service and Community Care Act 1990 does not define need; however, the practice guidance (Department of Health and Social Services Inspectorate, 1991) adopts the following definition:

> *The requirements of individuals to enable them to achieve, maintain or restore an acceptable level of social independence or quality of life as defined by the particular agency or authority.*

This supports a 'normative' approach to need. Bradshaw (1972, cited in Tanner, 1997) described 'normative need' as that defined by an expert or professional according to an agreed standard; individuals who fall short of this standard are considered to be in need. Tanner (1997, p450) argues that this normative approach, with need being defined by the 'particular agency or authority', leaves interpretation of need to local policy-makers. This not only allows central government to avoid unpopular decisions about which needs should be met but also creates inequity from one area to another. Arguably this continues despite eligibility criteria introduced by *Fair Access to Care Services* (DH, 2002) which has not addressed inconsistency between local authorities. For example, a local council can, when faced with diminishing resources, raise its eligibility criteria to a higher level.

What *Fair Access to Care Services* has introduced is the concept of 'eligible need'. *Fair Access to Care Services* guidance (DH, 2002) requires that an assessment of 'presenting needs' be undertaken and then eligible needs prioritised. Eligible needs are defined in terms of risk. The use of eligibility criteria with a focus on risk to determine allocation of resources has led to what Cambridge and Carnaby (2005) term 'critical need', where individuals in situations of high risk, or those attracting 'negative attention' from others, are more likely to receive resources. In assessing individuals' needs, there are numerous areas of risk which trigger eligibility for service provision, either because of vulnerability or challenging behaviour for example. However, as Cambridge and Carnaby (2005) identify, this approach is narrow and removes the potential for preventative work which may more effectively increase independence and quality of life for individuals with a learning disability.

Tanner (1997) suggests that eligibility criteria has also introduced an element of 'comparative need' (Bradshaw, 1972, cited in Tanner, 1997) – as 'service users are essentially in competition with one another for limited resources' their needs are weighed in comparison to that of others. This is evidenced in practice by the use of panels to allocate resources.

Rights

A rights-based approach rejects the focus on individual need to determine the allocation of resources because it reinforces 'inadequacy and inability' (Priestly, 1999, p211) rather than addressing structural inequalities. This view challenges the need for assessment at all, with the resources needed for independence and social participation being provided as a basic right. It is argued that community care policy with its emphasis on disabled people as customers and consumers does not address citizens' rights and may, Galpin (2009) suggests, in terms of personalisation, promote consumer rights over human rights.

Models of assessment

ACTIVITY **4.3**

- *What models of assessment do you use in practice?*

- *How are these evaluated in terms of effectiveness?*

- *How appropriate are these to your service user group?*

- *Do other professional groups use the same or different models?*

- *Does this make any difference to the assessment outcome?*

Means et al. (2003) emphasise that good assessment requires high levels of communication and interpersonal skills alongside a capacity for reflective practice rather than 'client processing' and form filling skills. In many local authorities, the systems used for documenting assessment is pro forma in style, which some might argue stifles creativity and a user perspective – especially where agency guidance regarding assessment with adults with a learning disability includes only the collection of information and identification of the service users' difficulties that prevent independent living. It does not guide workers to seek the person's strengths or views. This approach will only serve to strengthen oppressive practice in assessment. With its emphasis on 'identification of deficit of one kind or another' (Milner and O'Byrne, 2002), this style of assessment seems based on a medical approach to need where the cause of the 'problem' is seen as within people. Social influences, along with the causes of oppression, are neglected.

Using available paperwork, a checklist of functional abilities and deficits may be achieved; however, it can be a struggle for practitioners to reflect on what is important to the individual they are assessing – for example, individuals' needs in terms of the complex interaction between themselves and others and their environment which can be very important. It is important but sometimes difficult to avoid a procedural model of assessment where questions are asked and information is gathered according to the predetermined points on an assessment form. This model could lead to an individual with a learning disability to disengage from the process. Smale et al. (2000) point out that a procedural model does not address the issue of empowerment and involvement.

An exchange model of assessment, where the practitioner is not seen as an expert but as working in partnership with the individual, provides an approach to assessment that builds on an exchange of information between worker and service user. In this model of assessment, the underlying assumption is that:

> *People are, and always will be, the experts on themselves: their situations and relationships, what they want and need. (Smale et al. 2000, p137)*

This model enables the exploration of Bradshaw's (1972, cited in Tanner, 1997) two remaining categories of need that may define the services user's view of their own need. 'Felt need' is that need experienced by the individual themselves. 'Expressed need' refers to the need that is articulated by the individual and may not simply be the same as felt need expressed. Although an individual may communicate verbally, needs they are able to articulate are often more practical ones (cooking, cleaning, etc). Challenging behaviour or evidence of other emotional needs are more difficult to communicate. Practice guidance can limit the scope of an individual's participation in assessment according to their ability to express their needs.

Bradshaw (1972, cited in Tanner, 1997) suggests the definition of need will reflect the values and perspectives of those involved, therefore, finding ways to ensure the individual is fully involved in the assessment is essential if it is going to reflect an accurate picture of that individual's needs. Spending time with an individual in different settings – for example, making lunch together or going shopping – can assist in gaining a picture of more practical needs and at the same time build a relationship where an understanding of other less tangible needs could be developed.

Cambridge (1999) stresses the importance of getting to know people with learning disabilities so that assessment which is 'essentially about an understanding which takes place within the context of a relationship between the practitioner and the service user' (p406) can take place. The role of worker in the exchange model is to negotiate an agreement about how needs should be met and to ensure the service user remains central. It could be argued that the exchange model is not limited to assessment but should be extended throughout the care management process.

As has already been discussed, assessment is increasingly of risk rather than need. Yet, as Waterson (1998) highlights, risk assessment is barely mentioned in the official care management guidance (Department of Health and Social Services Inspectorate, 1991). The emphasis upon risk in health and social care can be seen by the large proportion of assessment documentation devoted to it, as opposed to the space allotted to something such as communication that is frequently so small one struggles to find it. Some joint risk assessment tools used when working with our health colleagues are essentially medical in focus, locating the problem within the individual and scoring the likelihood of a negative event. Sellars (2002) explains that while these types of forms can be said to be more objective, it is important that workers are able to record and explain *why* something is considered to be low or high risk.

Risk

ACTIVITY 4.4

- *How do needs, risk and rights interact in assessment?*
- *In your practice experience, do all professionals weight these elements equally? If not, how do you address this?*
- *How do you ensure you take a balanced approach?*

Assessment of risk is increasingly an integral feature of the process, particularly around areas of perceived vulnerability. Sellars (2002) points out that we all take risk decisions in everyday life and that we are able to do so because we have grown up with opportunities to make choices, take risks and weigh up the consequences. However, for people with learning disabilities, an emphasis on vulnerability means the risks of everyday life are considered to be greater, resulting in far fewer opportunities to make choices and the right to take risks is denied. Yet, Waterson (1998) suggests that achieving independence may involve taking risks. Pro formas and assessment 'tools' used by agencies may lead the practitioner and those providing support to focus mainly on the 'potential for harm' where thoughts around protection rather than positive risk taking dominate. Excessive protection could be seen as a contravention of individuals' human rights because it deprives them of choice and freedom. Waterson (1998) found that professionals tend to concentrate largely on risk avoidance while forgetting the potential benefits risk taking can bring. Consideration of an individual's mental capacity to make choices and decisions while being given the appropriate support to weigh up risks can assist in helping an individual to keep themselves safe rather than needing decisions of risk to be taken for them. An exchange approach to risk assessment assists practitioners to avoid a paternalistic approach with an emphasis on facilitating access to 'information, knowledge, definitions and expertise' (Braye and Preston-Shoot, 1995, p94).

Braye and Preston-Shoot (1995) explain that if workers are to practise in an empowering way, capacity rather than incapacity should be assumed. This is in line with current law presumption of capacity under the Mental Capacity Act 2005. Anti-oppressive practice will also recognise and address the impact that lack of opportunity has upon decision-making. Empowerment and enabling of informed choice is a theme that should underpin the care assessment/management process. Lloyd (2002) claimed that:

Social work will survive or fall according to its response to care management. (p167)

This could be true of contemporary practice, where good practice developed under care management is lost in the drive for modernisation, personalisation and transformation. As Mandelstam (2009) suggests, when discussing the harm that can come to individuals at the hands of local authorities when they apply:

Indiscriminate application of the mantra of 'independence, choice and control' in the context of self-directed care' – thus leaving some vulnerable adults at sometimes serious risk. (p42)

The care management process and personalisation

Cambridge and Carnaby (2005) identify two models of care management: the 'support coordination' model and the 'resource allocation' model. Support coordination is concerned with 'helping people get the help they need by organising paid or unpaid support' (Cambridge and Carnaby, 2005, p35). It could be argued that this is more in line with the original aim of care management as outlined in the practice guidance following the 1990 legislation and fits with personalisation. Care management was described as the process of tailoring services to individual needs and at its heart were key beliefs such as:

- needs-led assessment;

- more responsive services;

- partnership with users and carers;

- increased choice;

- improved opportunities for representation and advocacy;

- greater continuity of care;

- better integration of services between agencies.
  (Taken from *Care Management and Assessment: A Practitioner's Guide*, DH, 1991)

Care management, like personalisation, promised a fundamental departure from previous patterns of welfare delivery with needs-led assessments enabling more creative use of resources. However, others argue that this was merely rhetoric and in reality the National Health Service and Community Care Act 1990 introduced needs assessment because of concerns over large sums of money inappropriately spent on residential care (Davies et al., 2000). The requirement for need assessment was linked to the scarcity of resources, with a concern to focus the decreasing available resources towards those with the greatest need (Percy-Smith, 1996).

It was envisaged care management would promote rights and accomplishments such as those that John O'Brien proposed: community presence, community participation, choice, competence and respect (O'Brien, 1986, cited in Braye and Preston-Shoot, 1995) within learning disability services. However, as Cambridge and Carnaby (2005) identified:

> *Care management has shifted from a carefully constructed intervention and process, where care managers conduct a series of core tasks with limited caseloads, to a general policy instrument where care management has become demand driven, determined by administrative factors and constrained by resources. (p9)*

This shift is evidenced in the second model of care management identified by Cambridge and Carnaby (2005) – the 'resource allocation' model. Within this model the role of the care manager is more about the application of eligibility criteria and the rationing of resources. Lessons from care management might provide helpful guidance for practice in terms of personalisation.

Fair Access to Care Services and the introduction of eligibility criteria means that practitioners have to manage the conflict between the two models in everyday practice. In working with individuals with a learning disability, there are complex issues to consider – as a consequence of life experiences and often with difficulties in forming and sustaining relationships and with accepting support. A support coordinator model has the ability to facilitate a sense of control; for example, by developing the opportunity to explore different types of support and make a choice. Braye and Preston Shoot (1995) suggest that:

> *Maximising choice, where choice is genuine and significant, enhances control and is a form of empowerment. (p56)*

However, it can sometimes seem to practitioners that what the organisation demands is a resource allocator to administer checklists and eligibility criteria and reduce expenditure. This can be especially frustrating as it may conflict with social work values. For example, practice experience with individuals with a learning disability suggests they require consistent and enabling support. However, on occasions, practitioners report that they are put under pressure by the budget constraints to make a short-term placement because of the perceived cost of a package that might support an individual to be more independent in the community. From a practitioner perspective, this does not give proper consideration to the long-term cost to the individual of doing this and may lead to more expensive placements in the future. Funding for a required package can be achieved through an emphasis on risk but this can also compromise practice that is essentially meant to empower during the assessment process. Tanner (1997) found that to prove service users' eligibility, practitioners were 'obliged to stress the magnitude of their problems' (p451).

Valuing People and person-centred planning (PCP)

Cambridge et al. (2005) suggest that it is time to move away from the administratively driven resource rationing models and towards 'more empowering and person-centred interventions' (p1058). The strong emphasis on person-centred planning that was brought about by the White Paper *Valuing People* (DH, 2001b), and more recently *Valuing People Now* (DH, 2009), is beginning to impact upon care management practice with people with learning disabilities. *Valuing People* (DH, 2001b) and *Valuing People Now* (DH, 2009) identify person-centred planning as a priority for young people in transition. Person-centred approaches to planning services and support enables people with a learning disability to have more choice and control over their lives:

> *Person-centred planning is a process of continual listening and learning; focused on what is important to someone now, and for the future; and acting upon this in alliance with their family and friends. (Sanderson, 2000, p2)*

Person-centred planning addresses issues of exclusion that can be overlooked in the assessment process because it looks at the person's capacities and not their deficits. It does not assume that people need to change to gain inclusion but seeks to address the support they need to achieve the life they desire.

The listening involved in person-centred planning is good social work practice and can be used to understand an individual's choices and abilities. Person-centred methods also help to ensure that the individual remains central to the care management process. Funding, however, is an issue in ensuring person-centred planning for all individuals with a learning disability and can be heavily reliant upon the commitment of the individual's informal or unpaid support network to make their aspirations and plans a reality. Mansel and Beadle-Brown (2003) found evidence of an 'implementation gap', with person-centred plans becoming little more than 'a paper exercise' and having little impact on the lives of people with learning disabilities. While this might not be true of all, there is certainly still some way to go before all individuals with a learning disability benefit from person-centred planning. Mansel and Beadle-Brown (2003) further suggest that this is not because of a lack of understanding of how to implement person-centred planning but rather that a lack of resources undermines motivation to take planning seriously. More recent research has also suggested there is statistically no difference in some indicators of well-being between individuals with a learning disability in receipt of an IB and those who were not (Glendinning et al., 2008), suggesting real person-centred practice requires person-centred methods that look beyond government drives and initiatives.

Arguably the 'support coordination' model links well with person-centred planning. In fact Cambridge and Carnaby (2005) argue that if person-centred planning is to be effectively implemented, it must be underpinned by effective care management and that it is essential that the two do not operate as separate systems. While it is true that person-centred planning has a lot to offer care management, it can be argued that there is a risk that its effectiveness could be diluted and it could suffer the same fate as care management with increased caseloads and fewer resources leading to more administratively driven approaches.

Waterson (1998) highlights the impossible job that practitioners are faced with – that of minimising risks and empowering users with ever-decreasing resources. However, the picture is not completely negative. The assessment of individuals with a learning disability is complex and requires knowledge of social work methods and the use of social work rather than administrative skills. Lloyd (2002, cited in Adams et al.) highlights that service user responses in research showed that qualified social workers undertaking care management roles took service user involvement and empowerment seriously and were more likely to provide counselling. They also found evidence of 'a fight back by social work' with qualified social workers being responsible for the highest incidence of complex assessment and the guardians of the holistic assessment. Arguably, as social work practice evolves, in terms of *Safeguarding Adults* and Deprivation of Liberty Safeguards, for example, these skills will become more, not less, necessary to facilitate good practice.

ACTIVITY **4.5**

The context of social work practice is constantly evolving. Ask yourself and list:

• *The skills you already have that are transferable into new roles;*

• *The new skills you need to develop;*

• *How you will achieve this.*

Part one of this chapter has explored some of the factors that influence practice in contemporary social work in learning disability services. While not exhaustive, it provides a point from which practitioners can begin to analyse the context of their practice. Part two of this chapter now provides an opportunity to engage in analysis of real-life situations as an aide to develop skills by adopting a critical approach to practice.

Team activity: the facilitation of learning

Read the next section of this chapter and note what you think are the key issues.

- *Split the team into two groups and give them one case study each.*

- *Ask each team to make a note of what they think the key issues are and how they would work in this scenario.*

- *Ask both teams to give feedback of their thoughts to the whole group.*

- *Give feedback to the group on your findings having read the whole section, highlighting key points where the team and text agree and disagree.*

- *Ask the team to give constructive feedback on this activity and agree on future strategies to develop team learning.*

Practice analysis 1: working towards social inclusion

CASE STUDY *4.1*

Maria is a woman in her forties. She has a significant learning disability and some unusual behaviour. She lives in a large residential home and throughout her life has lived in many institutional settings – hospital and residential care – as she has no family. Over the years there have been many attempts by doctors and psychiatrists to attach a diagnosis to Maria, resulting in various 'labels' being applied to her. Maria has been described as 'demanding and difficult', requiring 'structure and routine'. She is also said to be 'obsessive'. There have been a number of incidents in her residential home and staff feel that Maria needs to be controlled before she will be able to engage in activities outside the home.

Rapley (2004) suggests that the pursuit of a diagnosis involves the acquisition of power and control over individuals, which might be the case for Maria. As a consequence, individuals accumulate a variety of labels which give a diagnosis and frequently include additional labels that describe behaviours; for example, 'obsessive', 'demanding', 'difficult' and 'challenging' – words which over time have probably been used to describe or label many people with learning disabilities. For individuals such as Maria, the responses produced in others by such negative labels may only serve to generate more of the behaviour associated with the label. Pierson and Thomas (2002) describe labelling as:

> *The process whereby people holding positions of power or influence sometimes attribute generalised negative characteristics to particular categories of individuals, tending to produce or amplify those behavioural characteristics attributed. (p251)*

Maria, for example, is described as 'obsessive' and 'demanding' and considered to require 'structure and routine'. Practitioners, therefore, may introduce routines; however, this may also become a regimented routine that can be introduced under the guise of independence and managing behaviour but actually functions as control which the individual may react against. This then perpetuates negative views of the individual. This type of approach has more in common with a medical view of disability, with the location of behaviour seen as an individual problem related to the functional limitations and impairment of the individual (Swain et al., 2003). This approach would not consider the environment or culture surrounding Maria as contributing to her difficulties.

Braye and Preston-Shoot (1995) explain that stereotyped and 'routinised' responses can lead to inflexible service provision which may undermine independence just as much as lack of support. This can result in not being able to tell how much of the behaviour of this nature is a result of her original impairment and how much is a consequence of care she has experienced as a result of being labelled. What is clear is that autonomy and independence can be significantly undermined.

Clements and Martin (2002) explain that different societies will vary in their values and in what is held up as ideal: those who do not fit this view will be marginalised and devalued. Some of Maria's behaviour contravenes accepted social norms for our society and is considered challenging and is labelled so. Concerns about, and responses to, Maria's 'challenging behaviour' and the risks associated with it can be so over-emphasised that she would not be offered ordinary opportunities that most of us take for granted; for example, going to the shops or out for a meal. The reason for a restrictive approach would be to protect her from 'the general public' because some of the things she may do could lead to misunderstandings, or protecting 'the public' from behaviour that may harm others. One might wonder at what point has Maria ceased to be a member of the public herself? Swain et al. (2003) highlight that a label of 'challenging behaviour' can invoke stereotyping and discriminatory assumptions about a person's worth that can be used to justify their exclusion.

Maria has no family contacts and her social world seems to be ever decreasing as services strive to protect her and others. Naylor (2006) identifies an 'absence of wider social networks as a factor that can increase the vulnerability of adults'. One way to address these types of issues might be to pursue opportunities to develop a wider range of relationships and activities in different settings; for example, adult education classes and use of community facilities to try out different activities so that she could find out which ones she enjoyed.

However, staff sometimes feel it is not possible to support individuals in community settings until the situation has improved and it can be difficult to see how things could improve while an individual such as Maria has such a restrictive lifestyle. One way in which change might be sought is via medication. This approach, however, links into the pervasiveness of the medical model and can be seen in requests for medication to resolve the situation. Mansell (1994) argues that we need to develop a more sophisticated understanding of challenging behaviour, viewing it as more than a 'bio-chemical malfunction' which would indicate a need for treatment, and rather as a socially constructed phenomenon produced by the interactions between individuals and their social and material environment.

Using this as a starting point, one could work with Maria and those who support her; for example, a community nurse to undertake a risk assessment. O'Sullivan (2002) suggests that a risk assessment should identify the danger, the likelihood of it occurring and the degree of harm that is likely if the danger occurs. In addition, he argues that a risk assessment should ask two other questions:

First, is the focus on risk justified and, second, does the method of risk assessment give a distorted representation? (O'Sullivan, 2002, p272)

Using multi-agency risk tools, currently employed by many local social services department and NHS trusts, specific risks can be seen in the context of an assessment of Maria's situation, including needs, likely triggers for behaviour and the benefit of taking the risk. Risk tools do have shortcomings in that they do not always emphasise the wishes and strengths of the service user (and in this way could give a 'distorted' analysis). However, the assessor can ensure that they include these points in the risk strategy to ensure that there is sufficient balance.

Practitioners sometimes find that perceptions of risk can be far greater than the reality and that almost all of the incidents of challenging behaviour giving rise to concern are environmental; for example, in Maria's case, it occurred within the residential home. This would lead to a risk strategy of providing increased activities outside the home and a risk management plan that focuses on giving choice and placing Maria in control of decisions regarding situations that she may find stressful while out. Alongside the risk assessment, the practitioner would seek to engage other professionals – for example, a psychologist for learning disability from the local National Health Service Trust – to establish if behaviour management plans would be able to assist Maria. Practice experience would suggest that sometimes what is required are more opportunities rather than behaviour management techniques as such.

In achieving a risk assessment based on choice and stressing Maria's capacities, one would be aiming to break what Tindal (1997) terms a negative cycle of consistently reinforced low expectations. One would work with staff to develop their confidence and skills so that they feel able to support individuals such as Maria to go out from the home and offer wider opportunities and choices, while also challenging some of the stereotypical thinking and responses that can become such a barrier to social inclusion.

This is only one factor that may contribute to the social exclusion of individuals with a learning disability. Thompson (2003) suggests that while it cannot be denied that individual prejudiced attitudes and behaviours play a part, it is a mistake to attach too much significance to the personal level as this is only one part of the picture. Practitioners need to reflect on the context of practice to understand that personal attitudes and responses of staff are part of a more complex situation.

Despite the introduction of risk assessment and management and regular reviews of plans, along with improved staff training and support, only a limited amount of success might be achieved in providing activities for an individual such as Maria in the community. Thompson (2003) identifies that discrimination at the personal or micro level is embedded within a cultural level. The culture within western society frequently views individuals with a learning disability in terms of stereotypes; for example, either an 'eternal child' in need of care and therefore dependent or as a 'threat' and in need of control (Clements and Martin, 2002). This can sometimes be demonstrated in the ethos of care providers in some residential settings; for example, practice experience suggests that some members of staff feel individuals with a learning disability 'don't need activities they need care'.

Discrimination and oppression at a cultural level owes much to the social and structural level that surrounds and envelopes it (Thompson, 2003). The exclusion from the community that some individuals such as Maria experience may be the result of the culture in a particular residential setting; however, this underpins the segregation of people with learning disabilities that can result from social and agency policies. For example, in response to the White Paper *Valuing People* (DH, 2001b), local initiatives have developed to support the 'new vision' for people with a learning disability to promote the 'rights, independence, choice and inclusion' discussed in the White Paper. However, these initiatives can still lead to segregation. For example, in some areas local provision for individuals with a learning disability who want to live more independently typically consists of a block of flats and a close of bungalows to provide accommodation. However, they are located all together and still separated from the rest of the community, with staff offices and toilets on site, and in one example, a catering project offers work opportunities but is sited in-between the day centre and the local social services office. Yet, this may appear justifiably protective when one considers cases such as Steven Hoskins and the 'Hounslow Case' (Community Care, 2008) where individuals with a learning disability located in the wider community were seriously abused, and in Steven's case, murdered (Flynn, 2006).

Cases such as these serve to highlight the dilemmas faced by practitioners and local authorities as they attempt to adhere to policy guidance contained in documents such as *Valuing People* (DH, 2001b) and *Valuing People Now* (DH, 2009) and remain aware of case examples where protection is an issue. While the practitioners and local authorities involved in the above cases may have considered themselves as anti-oppressive and sought to maintain a strong focus on individuals' rights, they still needed to understand the impact of cultural and structural oppression that seems 'sewn in' (Thompson, 2006) to the fabric of the service intended to support individuals such as Maria. Thompson (2003) reminds the practitioner that a broad perspective is required if a distorted picture of the situation is to be avoided, as happened in the Steven Hoskins case (Flynn, 2006).

Practice analysis 2: PCP, vulnerability and promoting independence

CASE STUDY 4.2

Joan is in her thirties. She lived with her sister and had no contact with adult services until her sister became terminally ill and she required an emergency placement. Joan is described as having an autistic spectrum condition. She requires time to make decisions, and also has a learning disability. Joan was moved from the emergency placement (a residential home) to her own tenancy with support for activities of daily living. Joan thrived and appeared to enjoy her independence. A short while after this her sister died and her uncle, with whom she had had no contact for about 20 years, telephoned the team asking to resume a relationship with his niece, whom he feels is unable to make decisions for herself due to her disability. A support worker arranged a meeting without fully consulting Joan. Later, Joan disclosed to her social worker that she had had a very difficult relationship with her uncle while she was growing up, experiencing what could be termed at best rough handling and at worst abuse.

McGlaughlin et al. (2004) stress the importance of people with learning disabilities being consulted about decisions which directly affect their lives. However, consultation alone is inadequate. Service users should, whenever possible, be given support to make their own decisions. For example, while there would be concerns about the potential risk to Joan, the issue of resuming contact with her uncle is a decision for Joan to make, if she is at all able, and one that practitioners should seek to enable her to make. The Mental Capacity Act 2005 requires that:

> *A person must be assumed to have capacity unless it is established that he lacks capacity (S. 1.2) and that 'all practicable steps to support the person to make their own decision are taken'.*

Clements and Martin (2002) identify that the impact of learning disability, for many people, is very significant in the area of communication: 'processing verbal input, expressing, verbally, thoughts, feelings and interpretations' which can affect decision-making. The practitioner's vital role would be to ensure that Joan is allowed the time she needed and was not rushed into decision-making. Work with Joan, whether it was with regard to her support needs, accommodation, day opportunities or contact with her uncle, would focus on enabling her to be in control of her life and make her own decisions.

Adams (1996, cited in Thompson, 2002) defines empowerment as:

> *the means by which individuals, groups and/or communities become able to take control of their circumstances and achieve their own goals. (p305)*

Thompson (2002) explains that empowerment can be seen as a specific strategy in work with service users but that it is also an important aspect of practice. All forms of good practice should aim in some way towards helping people to increase their level of control.

Joan was placed in a very vulnerable position when a support worker organised a meeting between Joan and her uncle without Joan's full collaboration. This may have been based on the support worker's assumptions about what was in Joan's best interests and her capacity to make choices and decisions:

> *The good intentions of caring staff are often a source of problems for the people who are concerned, problems that arise as a result of efforts to provide care standing in the way of people taking greater control over their lives. (Thompson, 2003, p130)*

Beyond this, Ife (2008) suggests from a human rights approach to practice that workers should be aware that making decisions in someone's best interests is fraught with ethical and moral difficulties and may actually compromise an individual's human rights.

Once aware of Joan's feelings about her uncle, the practitioner might support Joan to slow the process of contact with her uncle down to a pace that she was comfortable with to enable her to feel in control of the situation. Part of this process would involve undertaking a risk assessment with Joan. This would involve exploring with Joan the outcome that she wanted and the support she needed to achieve this. Tindal (1997) confirms that this is the basis of sound individual planning.

Stainton (2002) defines self-determination as choosing for oneself what one does or does not want to do, be or value. It can be argued that unless one has the ability to act upon one's choices, true self-determination is not achieved and this is another area where Joan might need support. Her uncle seems to hold a medical perspective with regard to Joan and her disability, which is not uncommon in families of those adults who are diagnosed as having a disability, taking the view that a diagnosis of autism automatically means that she cannot make her own decisions. It can take a considerable amount of time and energy to change this type of view. The support of an independent advocate to challenge this stereotype could be considered.

Individuals with a learning disability are particularly vulnerable to having their wishes disregarded if the decision they make is not seen by others as valid. Stainton (2002) emphasises that practitioners should be concerned with ensuring the opportunity to self-determination, rather than ensuring they achieve an outcome that others consider to be valid. However, this should not be seen as some special right that is accorded to individuals with a learning disability but rather as something anyone is entitled to achieve and, in this context, results in the prevention of discrimination and oppression. Joan may be able to make her own decisions given the time and space to do so. The difficult part for Joan would be getting other people to listen and to keep listening to her and acting upon her wishes. If a practitioner can achieve this, Joan's vulnerability will decrease as she decides on contact with her uncle which she controls.

It appears that Joan needs and accepts assistance with many of the practical aspects of daily living. However, the assistance she receives does not appear to detract from her view of herself as independent:

> *Independence, then, is not a question of not needing support; it is more a question of maximizing the control we have over our lives. (Adams, 1996, cited in Thompson, 2003, p108)*

Morris (1993) explains that in western industrial societies, the term 'independence' is commonly associated with self-reliance and the ability to do things for oneself. The assumption is made that those who cannot do things for themselves are 'dependent' and therefore assumed unable to control their lives. It may be that the support worker made this assumption regarding Joan's contact with her uncle and, as a consequence, placed Joan in a very vulnerable position. The assumption that dependence equates to the absence of independence is an example of what Fook (2002) describes as dichotomous thinking. She considers that these kinds of dichotomies can be constructed by practitioners themselves and can lead to rigid practice that is unhelpful to service users. Arguably, for Joan independence may not be about doing everything for herself or by herself but about being in control of the support that she has.

The perception of independence and dependence as being mutually exclusive presumes that individuals who require assistance have nothing to offer their community and denies their citizenship. Bates and Davis (2004) stress that the way in which individuals with learning disabilities are perceived by others has a significant impact on their social inclusion. If they are perceived as having no positive contribution to make, this limits the potential for forming wider relationships. Individuals with learning disabilities are frequently providers of support to other people – for example, partners, family members and friends; however, the 'caring' role of people with learning disabilities is rarely acknowledged. Dominelli (2004) suggests that when interdependency is acknowledged, it challenges the presumption that those who are in need of assistance, and therefore 'dependent', are unnecessary. Joan's sister may have been reliant on her for companionship and support and Joan might have felt the loss of this role since her death. However, she could find a new role in her life, if given appropriate support.

Valuing People (DH, 2001b) emphasises person-centred planning as the means whereby people with learning disabilities will be able to have more control over their lives. The ideal behind person-centred planning is one of:

> *continual listening and learning; focused on what is important to someone now,*
> *and for the future; and acting upon this in alliance with their family and friends.*
> *(Sanderson, 2000, p2)*

As a result of the considerable change in Joan's circumstances, she will probably have had a person-centred plan that support staff where she lived had helped her produce. Its existence, however, did not stop a staff member making decisions and taking control away from her. Without a commitment to 'person-centred action' (Emerson and Stancliffe, 2004) and a fundamental change in attitude, there is a danger of old practices merely being labelled person-centred.

Simpson (2002) warns that with such a strong emphasis on the individual, person-centred approaches can fail to recognise wider issues of inequality and discrimination, the causes of oppression and the main need of people with learning disabilities – 'for society to stop oppressing them'. Individuals who are labelled learning disabled are persistently viewed as vulnerable without proper consideration of contributing factors and there is a risk then of this becoming their fixed identity. Stainton (2002) reminds the practitioner that while definitions or labels such as 'learning disability' are constructs that help us to understand a 'phenomenon', they tell us little about the person behind the label and it should not be forgotten that such definitions are 'powerful tools' and can be used for 'good or ill'. It could be argued that the introduction of eligibility criteria has reinforced labelling with the requirement to have some form of label or diagnosis in order to gain access to scarce resources.

Thomas and Woods (2003) suggest that when services are restricted by rigid eligibility criteria, it will be difficult to gain access without 'various labels'. This leaves the practitioner with a difficult conflict to resolve. A fundamental value in social care is the respect for the unique individuality of each person; however, in order to obtain a service the emphasis is placed on the 'identification of deficit of one kind or another' (Milner and O'Byrne, 2002). The assessment format used in many local authorities has more in common with a medical model, beginning with a summary of the person's diagnosis and placing them in one category or another. The person is defined primarily in terms of their impairment. This format ignores wider social influences and defines service users in disempowered ways.

Morris (1993) explains that the need for assistance with activities of daily living has been translated into the need for 'care' and this can be seen reflected in the way 'care plans' are used to document support needs. It is argued that once assistance is seen as care, the disabled person is perceived as dependent on the carer and the carer then becomes the person in control. While caring is not always inappropriate or unwanted, there is a need for services to be much more critical with regard to their perspective on caring and recognise when it is more appropriate to concentrate on rights and empowerment (Thompson, 2003). It is a challenge to achieve a focus on rights and empowerment in assessment using the current format with its emphasis on eligibility and assessment of risk.

Smith (2005) suggests that eligibility criteria developed as a result of *Fair Access to Care Services* has produced a focus on crisis and has increased the vulnerability of people with learning disabilities with lower support needs, leaving them to struggle unsupported until a crisis means they qualify for services. The risks of social devaluation and exclusion are less likely to be seen as significant compared to risks from factors such as environmental hazards in the assessment of eligibility for people with learning disabilities. However, as this chapter has reflected, these risks will rarely be less important to the person themselves.

Pritchard (2001) reminds us that anyone may become vulnerable at some point in their lifetime for a variety of reasons and may need support. However, we are not all deemed to lack the ability for self-determination. Practice experience suggests once the label of learning disability is attached, the individual is perceived as 'not having capacity' to make decisions that are in their own best interests and thereby becomes vulnerable to the decision-making of others. People with learning disabilities are robbed of many of the resources that the rest of us rely on for decision-making and control in their everyday lives and this increases vulnerability. They are given less knowledge and information, less money, fewer choices and those that are made are often not respected. Being powerless and devalued, it is all too easy for powerful others to determine what happens in the lives of people with learning disabilities, to an extent that none of the rest of us would accept for ourselves (Clements and Martin, 2002).

Chapter summary

- Labels can serve to undermine person-centred practice when working with individuals with a learning disability.

- The NHS and Community Care Act 1990 provides a legislative foundation on which to build personalised services.

- Practitioners should be aware of different models of assessment and draw on the best of the care management process to support person-centred planning and practice.

- Person-centred planning and practice is able to promote social inclusion; however, practitioners need to be aware of how structural factors can lead to discrimination and oppression.

- Stereotypes can reduce practitioners' expectations of individuals with learning disabilities and lead to oppressive practice.

- Person-centred planning requires a commitment to person-centred action by all those who support the individual.

- Dependence and independence are not mutually exclusive concepts; indeed, individuals can be dependent, independent and interdependent all at the same time in different aspects of their lives.

- It is all too easy for powerful others to determine what happens in the lives of people with learning disabilities, to an extent that none of the rest of us would accept for ourselves.

FURTHER READING

Means, R., Richards, S. and Smith, R. (2008) *Community care policy and practice*, 4th edn. Basingstoke: Palgrave Macmillan.

This new edition has been updated to reflect recent shifts in community and social care while still providing the authoritative account of its historical development. Particular attention is paid to partnerships between health and social care, the regulation of social care, direct payments and individual budgets and user/carer empowerment.

Chapter 5

Direct payments and older people: developing a framework for practice

Elizabeth Burrow

ACHIEVING A POST-QUALIFYING SPECIALIST AWARD IN SOCIAL WORK WITH ADULTS

This chapter demonstrates how you might meet the GSCC specialist standards and requirements for post-qualifying social work education and training.

Legislation, social policy and social welfare

Social workers will need to extend and apply their knowledge and understanding of all relevant legal frameworks, social policies and social welfare principles within their particular area of practice. This includes all relevant legal and policy frameworks and the range of statutory responsibilities associated with working with adults. It also includes relevant legal and policy frameworks relating to mental health and the welfare of children and young people, together with the law relating to equality legislation and human rights.

Introduction

This chapter will discuss the socio-political context in which direct payments have developed. While direct payments were initially developed for service users with disabilities, this chapter will focus particularly on the implementation of direct payments with older people. Despite being the largest number of community care users, the number of older people using direct payments continues to be low, 'Just two per cent of the 650,000 eligible older people in England were receiving a payment in March 2006' (Samuel, 2007). Latest figures suggest council spending on direct payments in England for older people has risen to 3.6 per cent for the year 2006–2007; however, this still remains lower than for adults with physical disabilities, 24.3 per cent, and learning disabilities, 4.5 per cent (CSCI, 2009). Factors that influence practice in this particular area are discussed to try to establish, first, why take-up might be so low and, second, the relationship between direct payments, risk and anti-oppressive practice.

The socio-political context

ACTIVITY 5.1

- *Write a list of factors you think have influenced the development of direct payments for older people.*

- *How might your answers influence the implementation of direct payments in your practice with older people?*

The emergence of direct payments policy in the UK has been supported by a variety of factors. In the 1980s, following negotiations with disabled service users and activists, local authorities began to place financial resources under the control of individuals or small groups of disabled people, creating pilot schemes that involved 'indirect', 'third party' or 'brokerage' arrangements to channel public finance into self-directed personal support. These schemes gave rise to community-based organisations and user-led support groups who advocated for and contributed to the support of direct payments policy by disseminating information and knowledge to other potential users.

The implementation of the Disabled Persons (Services, Consultation and Representation) Act 1986 provided a legislative indicator of the government's drive to ensure local authorities engaged with service users when designing and delivering support services (Riddell et al., 2006). This was followed by the formation of a national Independent Living Fund (ILF) set up in 1988 to provide grants to disabled service users to purchase services to meet their identified care needs, thus demonstrating the level of demand and beneficial outcomes for service users who had more control over their care arrangements.

Originally older people were recipients of both 'indirect' payments and ILF payments prior to 1993 when the government closed the original fund and opened a new fund on a different basis called The Independent Living 1993 Fund. The introduction of the 1993 fund had a significant impact on older people as it excluded new applications from people aged over 66 years (Clark et al., 2004a).

Older people are, and have been, historically marginalised in society. Initially in the implementation of direct payments, older people were discriminated against as they were denied access. The Conservative government's initial decision to exclude older people was largely related to cost effectiveness, and a fear of their potential success, thus posing a possible risk to increased public spending. Issues about accountability and how to spend public money were also prevalent. As Clark (2006, p80) explains 'Older people are the biggest group of service users and should direct payments have proved an expensive experiment there would have been "major implications for public spending"' (Glasby and Littlechild, 2002, p77).

A move under a Conservative government in the 1980s from the principles of the post-war welfare state, dominated by bureaucratic administration and professional intervention, led to an increased emphasis on care management and dispersed welfare provision which reinforced a purchaser/provider split in a mixed economy of care (Clarke, 2001). 'A key

71

feature of the community care reforms of the 1990 NHS & Community Care Act was to encourage a greater range of providers, most explicitly to shift the balance from the statutory to the independent sector' (Davies, 1999, p329). Skidmore (1994) suggests 'the manifest function of community care is to provide a better quality of life. The latent function is to shift the responsibility for care provision' (p124).

The development of market forces and the 'mixed economy' of care increased competition between voluntary and private agencies, against which social service providers, and more recently users of direct payments, also now compete. These changes forced competition and highlighted the need for service providers to improve and develop their services and become more flexible and responsive to the needs of service users. One way in which government intended to meet these aims was through the introduction of direct payments.

The Community Care (Direct Payments) Act 1996 came into force in April 1997. It initially gave local authorities the 'power' but not a 'duty' to make direct cash payments (subject to assessment) to users of community care services. Age restrictions originally applied, with adults 18–65 who had a physical, sensory or learning disability, or various other illnesses – for example, HIV and AIDS – and people with mental health problems being eligible to receive direct payments.

However, 'New regulations in February 2000 rectified this age inequality and the power to make direct payments was eventually extended to older people, under the Labour government' (Monk, 2006).

Further developments in law shortly followed with the expansion of direct payments in July 2000 under the Carers and Disabled Children's Act to enable carers (including young carers) and people with parental responsibility for disabled children to access direct payments subject to assessment. The Health and Social Care Act 2001 later superseded the 1996 Act by converting the 'power' to a 'duty' when offering direct payments.

> *Since 8th April 2003 the power of authorities to make cash payments for care needs has been replaced by a duty to offer direct payments as an alternative to all service users and their carers who have been assessed as needing community care services or equipment and who meet the local authorities' eligibility criteria. (Davey et al., 2007, p4)*

> *Direct payments legislation is an important policy development for the disabled people's movement. It challenges disabling discourses of care and undermines cultural associations between disability and dependence. (Priestley, 1999, p204)*

The underpinning philosophy of direct payments is to give service users more control, choice and flexibility over their lifestyle. Direct payments have been campaigned for over many years by disability rights movements and are built on the foundations of a social model of disability. Their conception Clements (2000) suggests 'largely neutralised provisions made under the NAA 1948 s.29 (6) (a) which prohibits authorities from making cash payments to service users to enable them to procure their own care. Instead direct payments must relate to the user's own community care assessment and money must be spent on purchasing services to meet that need' (p142).

Those eligible for direct payments have now been extended by Section 146 of the Health and Social Care Act (2008) to allow 'other "suitable" people to consent and receive the payment on the disabled person's behalf' (Mandelstam, 2009, p53), including, in some circumstances, those users of the service without mental capacity. Suitable people may include family or friends.

Many local authorities have embraced direct payments, declaring, for example, the aim to increase direct payments across all client groups so that people using direct payments will form the largest proportion of all adults supported to live at home by 2010 (Davey et al., 2007). But there are variations between local authorities in their commitment to direct payments.

Research summary

Drawing on data from the project Disabled People and Direct Payments: A UK Comparative Perspective, this research suggests the potential for direct payments has only partly been realised as a result of very low and uneven uptake within and between different parts of the UK. This is accounted for in part by the resistance from some Labour controlled local authorities, which regard direct payments as a threat to public sector jobs. (Riddell et al., 2005)

ACTIVITY **5.2**

- *What is your employer's commitment to direct payments?*

- *How might this influence your practice?*

Personalisation and direct payments

Personalisation: A Rough Guide (SCIE, 2008)

What is personalisation?

Personalisation begins with person-centred planning, which provides the starting point for assessment and planning in social work practice to support individuals in achieving choice. A person-centred approach treats 'people as individuals with a unique history and personality, listens to their "voice" and recognises that all human life is grounded in relationships' (CSCI, 2008, p123). SCIE (2008) states

> *Personalisation means starting with the individual as a person with strengths and preferences who may have a network of support and resources, which can include family and friends. They may have their own funding sources or be eligible for state funding. Personalisation reinforces the idea that the individual is best placed to know what they*

need and how those needs can be met. . . . Personalisation is about giving people more choice and control over their lives. (p4)

How do direct payments relate to personalisation?

A direct payment represents one approach to delivering personalised social care.

A direct payment refers to a means-tested cash payment made in lieu of traditional social service provision to an individual who has been assessed as needing support. Those eligible for a direct payment can then arrange their own support. The money included in a direct payment only applies to social services.

How about IBs and personal budgets?

Other approaches used to deliver personalised social care include individual budgets (IBs) and personal budgets. IBs combine resources from different funding streams to which an individual is assessed as entitled. Currently these are local authorities, community equipment services, Disabled Facilities Grants, Supporting People, Access to Work and the Independent Living Fund. A personal budget, often used interchangeably with IBs, is the funding given to someone to meet their assessed needs. They can have money as a direct payment or can choose to manage it in different ways.

The role of the social work practitioner

ACTIVITY 5.3

- *What is the role of the professional in the context of direct payments?*
- *Can you identify any barriers that might restrict this role?*
- *Can you identify any factors that might support this role?*

Professional social workers occupy boundary positions between people who use services and a variety of views on their situations, along with different ideas about the choices they make and what they should do next (Adams, 2005). One view of the role of the social worker is to 'implement legislation on behalf of the state, as an arm of social policy' (Harris, 2005). Alternatively, it could be said that social workers need to navigate their way around government legislation using their knowledge and skills in a creative way to unpick legislative guidance and maximise independence and opportunities for service users and their carers. Keeping abreast of local developments and innovative work within private, independent and voluntary sectors is also central to be able to empower service users and their carers.

Professional discretion and values

Research summary

Lipsky's (1980, cited Ellis 2007) theory of 'street-level bureaucracy' suggests professionals are able to exercise discretion in the interpretation and implementation of policy and legislation in day-to-day practice. This notion is explored by Ellis (2007) in her research on social work practice and direct payments suggesting 'although direct payments are governed by the same eligibility criteria as those governing direct services, implementation studies of direct payments legislation have consistently highlighted the scope of front line discretion in determining access' (p408).

Ellis' (2007) research suggests the modernisation of social care both challenges and supports Lipsky's theory as practitioners are encouraged to increase the uptake of direct payments while also managing scarce resources leading to informal rationing, which could operate outside the eligibility criteria. As direct payments now form part of the bigger personalisation agenda, along with the introduction of individual budgets, Ellis (2007) concludes 'Unless entitlement to individual budgets is strengthened by far more extensive advocacy and support services, the conditions which allow, even encourage, front line social workers to behave as "street level bureaucrats" are unlikely to disappear' (p419).

Social work practice, therefore, arguably carries with it a certain level of professional discretion. One way in which practitioners attempt to mediate between the subjective self in practice and the objective professional is to ensure one adheres to social work values. The core values of social work remain fairly consistent; however, to adhere to them requires awareness and commitment. For example, practitioners face the challenge of meeting government performance indicators and frameworks which support the continued extension of schemes such as direct payments to older people while some research indicates this type of approach might not be beneficial for older people who use services (Glendinning et al., 2008).

Social work values and practice

Beckett and Maynard (2005) suggest a value system is an enduring organisation of beliefs concerning preferable modes of conduct or end states of existence along a continuum of relative importance, and go on to suggest 'beliefs of these kind are an important cornerstone of our existence, acting as a filter which defines the things we accept or reject. Value systems inform our actions, they are part of the "emotional mobilisation" that makes us jump one way as opposed to another. They shape the way we think, the judgements we make, the perceptions we hold about people, and the companions we choose to spend our time with' (p8).

Therefore, professional values shape professional practice. The Code of Ethics for Social Workers (BASW, 2002) provides the values and principles on which practice should be built.

Social work is committed to five basic values:

- Human dignity and worth;

- Social justice;

- Service to humanity;

- Integrity;

- Competence.

Social work practice should both promote respect for human dignity and pursue social justice, through service to humanity, integrity and competence.

ACTIVITY **5.4**

How do values influence your practice with direct payments and older people?

Direct payments in practice

A key theme of research into direct payments and their take-up is the role of the social worker, their knowledge, understanding and attitude towards direct payments (Carr and Robbins, 2009). It has been suggested that for direct payments to work social workers need to relinquish control to service users to redress power imbalances. Some studies have suggested social workers fail to offer direct payments to older people because they believe that older people will not want the responsibility associated with managing the payments (Hasler et al., 1998; Clark et al., 2004a; Leece and Leece, 2006; CSCI, 2009). Training and support, or a lack of it, has been cited as a key factor, with claims that people are not making informed decisions to reject the idea of direct payments but that it is social workers who are depriving them of access to direct payments by failing to provide support and information (Tanner and Harris, 2008). Alternatively, it has been suggested workers are over-emphasising the risks and responsibilities of direct payments, which could exacerbate people's fears, rather than providing encouragement and support to take the direct payment option (CSCI, 2004b).

However, direct payments are just one alternative in the array of available community care services. Part of the role of the social worker is to assess people's needs against the eligibility criteria and work in partnership with service users and carers, their families and other professionals to support people to make the right choices to meet their individual needs. Direct payments do have the potential to be used creatively and flexibly to meet people's needs but this should not detract from the fact that some people just want, or even need, to be looked after and that personalisation of services is not wholly dependent on the acceptance of a direct payment (CSCI, 2009). One might also consider in the management of crisis situations, when emergency intervention is required or with additional pressures – for example, when planning for hospital discharge – it can be argued that direct payments can and do struggle to offer that 'quick fix' solution and therefore it might not then be appropriate to even consider a direct payment at this stage. However,

> *Good social work practice should include giving clear information and advice to older people about the options available, providing access to effective support and building in opportunities for them to review decisions in the light of changing circumstances. (Tanner and Harris, 2008, p108)*

It is no surprise that direct payments, along with all other types of service provision, have advantages and disadvantages. The development of a more consistent framework, where direct payments are recognised as a component of social care as opposed to a competitor, could play a role in changing the expectations of professionals, service users and providers, so that all services become more responsive to the needs and aspirations of their potential and actual users (Lyon, 2005).

A report by the CSCI (2004b) uncovered barriers to the take-up of direct payments. A UK comparative study about disabled people and direct payments conducted by Riddell et al. (2006) focused on how direct payments have been implemented across the UK, concentrating on how regional differences and the implementation of policy within the context of devolution in England, Scotland, Wales and Northern Ireland can support future policy development. Both pieces of research identified 'policy ambiguity' as a problem for government to overcome in order to remove the potential for different interpretations by local authorities. Clear guidelines were requested to enable staff to fully understand the systems.

Terminology was also found to be confusing to some people as the same vocabulary is used by the Department of Work and Pensions in relation to benefit payments. Inconsistencies between the intention of the legislation and local practice, and unnecessary and over-bureaucratic paperwork were also cited. Evidence was also found that care packages involving a direct payment are often subject to additional levels of assessment and checks compared to direct service provision.

More recent research suggests while direct payments are more readily available and understood by practitioners and older service users alike, barriers still exist (CSCI, 2009; Carr and Robbins, 2009).

However, despite these difficulties the drive for direct payments continues to remain strong from both government and service user groups. Although historically direct payments can involve additional time and paperwork to set up, once in operation with the appropriate support they can be a highly effective way of delivering a personalised service, with minimal disruption or complaints, as control rests with the service user.

> *While we recognise that we cannot make people choose direct payments, there is national evidence that suggests that if we present the direct option positively and*

concisely, and make the process of setting up and administering them as simple as possible, then more people are inclined to try them. Once people embark on direct payments very few revert to direct service provision. (Davey et al., 2007, p6)

Direct payments are central to the government's agenda for the modernisation and transformation of adult social care, yet there are some concerns regarding potential risks and a reduction in rights for those who use direct payments to manage and develop personalised care pathways.

Risk and direct payments

ACTIVITY **5.5**

Risk and direct payments

- *Have you identified potential risks that might exist for individuals who use direct payments?*

- *How do you manage those risks, or enable others to manage those risks, to promote maximum autonomy within a protective framework of practice?*

As service users use direct payments to employ their own personal assistants (PAs) to deliver their care needs, issues around who is monitoring and regulating this sector of care providers, and whether this leaves vulnerable members of society open to abuse, have been raised. Carmichael and Brown (2002) state 'The introduction of direct payments is complex and requires practical operational changes, a shift in approach to the concepts of risk and control, and a challenge to the culture of direct service provision' (p120). While, Askheim (2005) suggests that:

> *The importance of empowerment for the users has to be balanced against the responsibility the welfare state has for all its inhabitants and for protecting them against misfortunes and risks, of which users might not realise the consequences due to, for example, cognitive limitations, lack of life experiences or mental imbalance. (p34)*

Scourfield (2007) suggests direct payments pose challenges for practitioners as the level of regulation of the standards of care provided is variable, going on to argue that there is an unresolved ambiguity over accountability as those employed through a direct payment are less regulated than other social care providers. This suggests to Scourfield (2007) that direct payments may represent the state 'writing itself out of its traditional responsibilities' (p118); however, it may also represent a genuine attempt to shift the balance of power from the state to service users in a more meaningful manner.

As always, the assessment and management of potential risks is a complex task and raises issues about accountability and responsibility. On the one hand, the local authority through the monitoring and review process regulates direct payments; however, this is largely concerned with auditing the money, ensuring it is not being misappropriated and is equivalent to meet assessed needs. On the other hand, whom the service user employs is generally their choice and responsibility. Regulation and training of personal assistants is not obligatory, evidence of qualifications or certification is discretionary. This is the risk employer's take. However, as Hasler states, 'many current users cherish their right to use informal recruitment and unregulated staff' (2003, p23).

Leece (2004) offers two differing perspectives to the debate of employing informal or unregulated staff. First, that employing friends or relatives that may not have naturally entered the care workforce could help improve the recruitment shortfalls in the care sector generally; and second, in contrast, that the use of unregulated schemes where disabled people employ PAs from the 'grey' labour market who are, for example, unemployed or migrant workers, poses both risks to employer and employee. This limits protection for both parties as employers loose the facility to run meaningful checks on their employee's background and workers can lack employment protection.

Therefore, the dilemma still stands, if abusive behaviour occurs, who will be deemed accountable? The government or local authority for not putting stricter regulations and support services in place? The social worker for promoting and assessing the service user as being eligible for direct payments? Or the service user who chose to employ the personal assistant now perpetrating the abuse?

> *Paradoxically, while the service of direct payments is monitored, reviewed and audited, the actual services purchased with the direct payments are neither monitored nor regulated. The direct payments user is a strange hybrid construction being a 'citizen-as-consumer-as-service-user-as-employer' (see Spandler, 2004, p189). They are both in control and controlled at the same time. They are 'set free' but responsibilised through audit mechanisms. As Power (1994) puts it, 'audit is the control of control' (cited in Rose, 1999, p154). Should evidence of abusive behaviour by unregulated personal assistants emerge in the future one wonders whether the victim might, on some level, be held responsible. (Scourfield, 2005, p481)*

In contrast to this Spandler (2004) argues that agreeing and enforcing standards of care may limit the innovative and creative use of direct payments that challenge decisions around existing standards and practices. The greater status and training personal assistants receive could potentially threaten the balance of power and control that direct payments afford their users in the first place.

It is argued that direct payments require local authorities to make a cultural shift in the way risk and control are approached, with an acceptance that users have the right to take risks and achieve a greater degree of responsibility and power (Leece, 2003, 2004); however, there also needs to be some discussion on how those individuals who exercise their right to take such risks achieve the same level of protection as those users of services who decide not to engage in direct payments.

> **Research summary**
> - *Research shows that older people tend not to complain and are most likely to express satisfaction (Bauld et al., 2000).*
>
> - *Older people may receive a poor service and have unpleasant experiences but do not want to make a stressful situation worse by complaining about a service or lack of care that they perceive as unalterable (Gorman, 2005, p163).*

Developing good practice

ACTIVITY **5.6**

Developing good practice
- *Make a list of what you feel supports good practice in working with older people who choose a direct payment.*
- *Is there anything else your organisation could do to support and develop good practice?*

The importance of established robust direct payments support services are widely recognised as being a key element to making direct payments work for the majority of service users, especially for groups such as older people. Research around direct payments and older people conducted by Clark et al. (2004a) found support services that offer service users guidance and information, assistance with recruitment, wording adverts, help with advertising and contractual arrangements are all deemed valuable. Those schemes offering payroll services have been particularly welcomed, as managing the finances are an area that older people are most worried about. Access to good telephone support was felt by the older people surveyed to be crucial, 'especially when you are on your own and having difficulty' you need someone to talk to who understands what you need. The opportunity for peer support and to share ideas and examples of good practice is again thought to be beneficial. Where support services held a register of PAs, older people who had access to the register were appreciative, and those whose schemes did not offer this facility thought it was a good idea, and a relatively safe means of recruitment.

Direct payments also have the ability to offer Black and Minority Ethnic people a culturally sensitive and responsive service, by using them in innovative ways to secure culturally relevant support. However, as Tanner and Harris (2008, p107) explain:

> *It seems that additional barriers are faced by Black and Minority Ethnic people, who are considerably underrepresented among direct payments users, despite the potential of direct payments to deliver a more culturally responsive service (Butt et al., 2000).*

Again, the need for appropriate and sensitive support services is seen as an essential pre-requisite to achieving success with direct payments for Black and Minority Ethnic people, and should not be viewed as a panacea for filling gaps or deficiencies in existing service provisions (Clark et al., 2004a).

Research summary: accessing culturally relevant services

Research from the Joseph Rowntree Foundation (Clark et al., 2004b) found Somali older women were able to secure culturally sensitive services where statutory agencies were unable to provide Somali-speaker care assistants. Having someone who can speak the same language was crucial in enabling the Somali women to be in control and determine what was done for them. They no longer had to rely solely upon family members for support, and their family relationships improved.

However, having access to an accountancy service to deal with banking and administrative requirements was essential in overcoming the language and literacy barriers faced by the older women. A link between Somali community workers and the direct payments support service helped to bridge the information gap between social services and the community, as well as give older people access to direct payments.

While direct payments may prove empowering for some individuals, practitioners need to ensure they do not lose sight of the individual and acknowledge that direct payments might not meet the needs of all service users. The drive to increase the uptake of direct payments could obscure this fact in a bid to enable local authorities to meet performance management targets. Therefore, practitioners are required to be critically reflective in practice to ensure that practice is person-centred, anti-oppressive and consistent with their professional values.

A framework for practice: anti-oppressive practice

ACTIVITY 5.7

- *What is oppression?*
- *How do you ensure your practice is anti-oppressive?*

This approach helps support practice that meets government's desire to modernise social care through personalisation using approaches such as direct payments and IBs, and enables social work practitioners to work within an appropriate professional value base.

Dominelli (2002) defines anti-oppressive practice as:

- A form of social work practice which addresses social divisions and structural inequalities in the work that is done with service users or workers. Anti-oppressive practice aims to provide more appropriate and sensitive services by responding to people's needs regardless of their social status.

- The embodiment of a person-centred philosophy, an egalitarian value system concerned with reducing the deleterious effects of structural inequalities upon people's lives; a methodology focusing on process and outcome.

- A way of structuring social relationships between individuals that aims to empower service users by reducing the negative effects of hierarchy in their immediate interaction and the work they carry out.

Core assumptions of anti-oppressive practice

- Practitioners must recognise multiple forms of oppression and all forms should be acknowledged as harmful (Thompson, 2001).

- Oppression arises from unequal power across social divisions.

- Social divisions shape practice, and, further, we can reduce the disempowering effects of these differences by critical reflection on our position within these social structures.

Thompson (1998) states 'there is no middle ground; intervention either adds to oppression (or at least condones it) or goes some small way towards easing or breaking such oppression' (p11). Practitioners should adopt an ongoing critically reflective stance so as to avert, as far as possible, replicating oppressive social relations in practice. There are multiple layers of oppression. Anti-oppressive practice requires practitioners to constantly reflect on ways in which social structures interact with personal levels of oppression. For example, where the drive to increase uptake in direct payments to meet performance targets might leave an individual at risk.

Principles of anti-oppressive practice

Healy (2005) provides five practice principles that can provide a useful framework for practitioners to develop anti-oppressive practice.

Practice principle 1: critical reflection on self in practice

This approach demands reflection on the practitioners' own biographies, especially how membership of particular social divisions shapes practice and how this might affect their capacity to truly empathise with and understand service users' experiences. This could be used to address research that suggests social workers' perception on direct payments and the nature/abilities of older people affects their implementation.

Practice principle 2: critical assessment of service users' experiences of oppression

This approach argues that, in our analysis of service users' oppression, it is important to consider the impact of major social divisions such as ethnicity, class and gender, as well as other divisions such as age, mental health and employment status. For example, how might older people's experiences of being viewed as an 'old' person impact on their ability to engage in direct payments? Mead (1934) believed individuals derive pictures of themselves through what we learn from others' pictures of us. How others view us impacts on how we view ourselves. We then build a continuous picture of ourselves out of our interactions with others. Therefore, if an older person has been exposed to negative pictures of older people, this might affect their belief in their ability to engage with direct payments.

Practice principle 3: empowering service users

Anti-oppressive approaches to empowerment seek to overcome the cultural, institutional and structural, as well as personal, obstacles to service users taking greater control of their lives. This could include the following.

- Identify the skills of service users, and help to develop these further in order to enable the service user to gain confidence; for example, in identifying barriers that might prevent using a direct payment and addressing them.

- Ensure that service providers are aware of anti-oppressive practice and encourage service users to be involved in decision-making around the delivery and commissioning of services; for example, by exploring a range of options, including direct payments.

Practice principle 4: working in partnership

Anti-oppressive practice involves a commitment to genuine partnership working with service users. In the context of direct payments, this requires open and clear communication of the statutory limitations and responsibilities and ways in which these might be challenged. Clarity of communication is also required to ensure partnership working, which includes the use of jargon free language and clear written agreements, drawn up by both service user and practitioner.

Practice principle 5: minimal intervention

Anti-oppressive theorists adopt the principle of minimal intervention; this means that practitioners should aim to intervene in the least intrusive and least oppressive ways possible. Therefore, while there might be some risk this should not mean a direct payment will not be offered. However, it is recognised within this approach that in high-risk situations social workers may need to enact social control. This means more focus on early intervention with the primary aim of preventing the escalation of risk of harm to service users.

- Can you use Healy's five practice principles to develop a framework to support your work with older people and direct payments?

- Could this framework be incorporated in your team?

Direct payments: implications for the future

Service provision in general is likely to change and this could impact greatly on directly provided services, such as day care. If service users are choosing the direct payment option instead of attending a local day centre, will it be a viable option to continue running the day centre services, or does this mean that day care services will need to be redesigned completely, and if so, how will this impact on service users? Research by Scope indicated 'push–pull' factors affecting disabled people's decision to apply for direct payments. While some services users were being 'pulled' towards direct payments by the benefits they offer around control, choice and flexibility, other people were being 'pushed' towards direct payments, as they were dissatisfied with the standards of direct service provision they were receiving.

> The focus on the undeniable changes in welfare services, and how they are organised, managed and delivered diverts attention from the unchanging realities of being poor, being a lone parent, experiencing mental health problems, becoming older or living in a society which discriminates against people who are different, whether through class, age, gender, ethnicity disability or other social divisions. (Adams, 2002, p9)

'Discrimination does not exist in the prejudiced attitudes of individuals but in the institutional practices of society' (Alcock et al., 1999, p261). 'Existing inequalities are maintained through processes of discrimination that have the effect of allocating life chances, power and resources in such a way as to reinforce existing power relations' (Thompson, 1998, p11). Direct payments are a way of breaking down these barriers and giving service users the control, choice and flexibility they deserve and require for leading an independent lifestyle.

As Lyon (2005) suggests:

> Rather than using direct payments to justify avoiding service development, the challenge for local authorities is to support service development that incorporates principals of flexibility, choice and control as the norm for all styles of service provision. (p250)

Widely held assumptions and values about welfare provisions can be questioned by the implementation of direct payments practice which has disrupted traditional divisions between left and right political discourses. The focus of New Labour and their development of a Third Way are based on a mixture of New Right, New Labour and welfare user movement ideologies and demands where opportunity, rights and responsibility go hand in hand (Spandler, 2004). Under New Labour, elements of the reforms instigated by the previous Conservative government have been developed and extended rather than radically changed. A new emphasis on central regulation and control to monitor and enforce standards has been adopted, while a belief in the mixed economy of care has been retained. (Tanner and Harris, 2008).

A key principle of the government Green Paper *Independence, Well-being and Choice: Our Vision for the Future of Social Care for Adults in England* (DH, 2005) was that 'everyone in society has a positive contribution to make to that society and that they should have the right to control their own lives'. This theme continued in the following White Paper *Our Health, Our Care, Our Say* (DH, 2006) and the concordat *Putting People First* (DH, 2007b). However, as Tanner and Harris (2008) discuss, the idea that it is possible to improve the independence and well-being of older people at the same time as achieving cost savings, at least in the short and medium terms, is questionable.

Research summary

Britain's population is ageing and people are living longer than ever before. The largest group of adult users of social care is people aged 65 and over – an age group that is predicted to increase by 43 per cent by 2026. Demographic trends and people's expectations pose an urgent challenge to everyone involved in developing social care policy, in planning and delivering services, and inspecting and regulating those services. (CSCI, 2004a)

Increasing the use of direct payments was proposed within the Green Paper *Independence, Well-being and Choice* (DH, 2005) as a way of responding to these demographic changes. Alongside this was the recommendation to introduce individualised budgets. These suggestions were then taken forward in the White Paper, *Our Health, Our Care, Our Say* by the Department of Health in 2006.

> *Individual budgets offer a radical new approach, giving greater control to the individual, opening up the range and availability of services to match needs, and stimulating the market to respond to new demands from more powerful users of social care. (DH, 2006b, para. 4.30, cited in Tanner and Harris, 2008, p108)*

An evaluation of pilot projects for individual budgets suggests older people reported lower levels of psychological well-being than those who did not engage in individual budgets. Going on to state 'Information from qualitative interviews with service users and their proxies indicated that many older people supported by adult services do not appear to want what many of them describe as the "additional burden" of planning and managing their own support' (Glendinning et al., 2008, p19).

> *Globally, society is becoming increasingly commodified and marketised and people are recognised primarily as buyers and sellers in an increasingly dehumanised and alienated marketplace. (Spandler, 2004, p202)*

The ability to communicate and work jointly with others using a personable approach is therefore a key skill for social workers to possess to enable effective partnerships to be formed. 'Care in the community should be a partnership where seniority is gradually handed over to the client through empowerment' (Skidmore, 1994, p102). The social worker will obviously maintain their professional status; however, their role will often be to work in closer partnership with the service user and others to enable a shift in greater control for the service user. 'The concept of working together in partnerships and across role boundaries towards goals which may have to be negotiated provokes a very different image from that of the individual autonomous professional fixing something that has gone wrong' (Brechin et al., 2000, p37). As Leece and Bornat (2006) suggest:

> With subsequent labour government support, direct payments have now become a change agent in social care provision, with self-assessment being identified as a natural precursor. The implications for service providers are as dramatic as they are for service users. (p4)

To achieve partnership, the practitioner would prefer service users were able to consent to (choose, wish, want) a direct payment to fulfil the 'willing' part of the guidance; different methods of communication need to be taken into account. To be deemed 'able' pertains to their ability to manage the service, which can be done with the assistance of a third party. Assistance is generally of key importance for most service users when determining their 'ability to manage' a direct payment, especially if they have impaired cognitive abilities or challenging behaviour. Control is also very closely linked with being able to manage; a service user can have control over their service if they are able to make choices and decide, for example, about who supports them or whether they go to the gym or college instead of the day centre. They do not need to be able to take on all the responsibilities of employing their own personal assistant, such as managing the money and paying wages, tax, and national insurance; assistance can and ought to be used to support and facilitate the user's choice.

> Authorities should also ensure that their own procedures do not impair the user's ability to manage. Keeping record-keeping simple – with requested information being no more than the minimum necessary to ensure accountability – is one way to do this. (Hasler et al., 1998, p6)

Direct payments have come a long way since their conception in 1996. Evidence from research shows that individuals want to choose their social care – three-quarters (73 per cent) say a person requiring social care should be able to choose their services and be given money by the government or council to pay for them, rather than have the government or local authority decide (Commission for Social Care Inspection, 2004a, 2009).

As discussed, there are numerous factors that influence the take-up of direct payments. 'The quality and success of care-giving relationships often depend on the extent to which carers and the persons being cared for can negotiate the boundary between dependence and independence' (Ahmed, 2000, p23).

> Direct payments can change social care for older people just as it has done for younger disabled people. But making this a reality must involve challenging the notion that older people are passive recipients of social care and recognising that they can indeed 'create and manage their own services'. It also demands that SSDs appreciate the ethos of independent living that underpins direct payments. (Clark et al., 2004a)

> **Report findings: the state of social care in England 2007–8**
> *The task must surely be to ensure that all of those who want choice, flexibility and control are supported in their endeavours, even – or perhaps especially – when their needs are complex and their capacity to communicate their preferences is extremely limited.*
>
> *This is a human rights issue and human rights principles and approaches should underpin every aspect of the steps to personalise support to people with multiple and complex needs. This includes commissioning, service delivery and ensuring person-centred practice. (CSCI, 2009, p156)*

Chapter summary

- Direct payments are integral to the modernisation of adult social care services. They provide a tool which enables practitioners, service users and carers to achieve personalised care provision.

- Despite being the largest number of community care users, the number of older people using direct payments continues to be low.

- A key theme of research into direct payments and their take-up is the role of the social worker, their knowledge, understanding and attitude towards direct payments.

- It has been suggested for direct payments to work, social workers need to relinquish control to service users to redress power imbalances.

- Some studies have suggested social workers fail to offer direct payments to older people because they believe that older people will not want the responsibility associated with managing the payments.

- Direct payments are central to the government's agenda for the modernisation and transformation of adult social care, yet there are some concerns regarding potential risks and a reduction in rights for those who use direct payments to manage and develop personalised care pathways.

- The importance of established robust direct payments support services are widely recognised as being a key element to making direct payments work for the majority of service users; especially for groups such as older people.

- Anti-oppressive practice is practice that meets the government's desire to modernise social care through personalisation, using approaches such as direct payments and IBs. It also enables social work practitioners to work within an appropriate professional value base.

FURTHER READING

Glasby, J. and Littlechild, R. (2009) *Direct payments and personal budgets: putting personalisation into practice.* 2nd edn. Bristol: The Policy Press.

Crawford, K. and Walker, J. (2008) *Social work with older people.* 2nd edn. Exeter: Learning Matters.

Chapter 6

Transformation: a future for social work practice?

Diane Galpin

ACHIEVING A POST-QUALIFYING SPECIALIST AWARD IN SOCIAL WORK WITH ADULTS

This chapter demonstrates how you might meet the GSCC specialist standards and requirements for post-qualifying social work education and training.

Legislation, social policy and social welfare

Social workers will need to extend and apply their knowledge and understanding of all relevant legal frameworks, social policies and social welfare principles within their particular area of practice. This includes all relevant legal and policy frameworks and the range of statutory responsibilities associated with working with adults. It also includes relevant legal and policy frameworks relating to mental health and the welfare of children and young people, together with the law relating to equality legislation and human rights.

Introduction

The organisation and delivery of social work services across the United Kingdom has seen significant changes as government seeks to restructure the process of assessment, service development and delivery to reform adult health and social care. Modernisation, personalisation and transformation (MPT) provide the structural frameworks that support social work practitioners in implementing reform. Social work should be thriving as a centralised 'one size fits all' approach gives way to an agenda premised on personalisation and transformation, where users of services are supported to take control of, and develop, their own personalised care pathways utilising tools such as person-centred planning, individual budgets and direct payments. However, research would seem to suggest social work is, at best, surviving rather than thriving under MPT. This chapter will critically analyse the context in which MPT has developed, suggesting an exploitation of ambiguity in meaning in policy and guidance, blended with a process of depoliticisation, has led to increasing disillusionment within the social work profession. While MPT appears congruent with the core values of social work, its implementation has been characterised by an individualistic approach to practice that obscures issues of structural discrimination and oppression, and reduces practitioners' consciousness of social work as a human rights activity. The chapter concludes that transformation of adult social care requires a commitment to human rights from both social work professionals and organisational leaders if social work is going to make a positive contribution to adult social care in the future.

The reform of the public sector

MPT are central features in the government's drive to reform the public sector. They are interdependent and form the structural framework on which the whole of the public sector will develop in the future (National School of Government, 2007).

Modernisation

Policy briefing

Modernisation has been central to public sector reform and has outlined the direction of travel for the future of the public sector. In adult social care, several documents underpin the current context of practice and provide some insight into the future of social work practice.

Modernising Social Services (DH, 1998a)

This represents one of the key documents presented by government of its agenda to ensure the delivery of effective social services. The document identified five areas of particular concern:

- *protection (adult and child services);*

- *coordination (across and between agencies);*

- *inflexibility (services designed to meet the needs of the agency, not the individual);*

- *clarity of role (public has no understanding of who provides what and where);*

- *consistency (huge differences in standards and levels of services available across geographic areas and within departments).*

Three pathways were introduced that would act as benchmarks for change:

- *promoting independence;*

- *improving consistency;*

- *convenient user-centred services.*

Legislation, policy and guidance was introduced to help achieve these benchmarks. These include: No Secrets (DH, 2000), Single Assessment Process, National Service Frameworks, Valuing People (DH, 2001b), Fair Access to Care Services (DH, 2002) and Community Care (Delayed Discharges) Act (2003).

The modernisation agenda evolved after the election of New Labour in 1997 as a series of Green and White Papers and policy guidance were published to outline plans for the reform of the public sector (DH 1997, 1998a, 1998b, 1998c, 1999b). Six key principles underpinned the modernisation process:

- greater integration between health and social care;

- making sure public service users, not providers, are the focus of provision;

- greater choice for users of services;

- right to public sector provision balanced against individual responsibility to contribute to support oneself and the wider community;

- value for tax payers' money by utilising the free markets in service development and provision, via the private, voluntary and independent sectors;

- a target-focused approach to address concerns around the efficiency, effectiveness and economy of the public sector.

These principles have provided the conditions in which personalisation has developed.

ACTIVITY **6.1**

- *Look at the six principles above. Can you identify any further factors that have underpinned the modernisation process?*

- *Have these key principles changed the experiences of service users and carers in adult social care provision?*

- *If so, how?*

Personalisation

Policy briefing

Following the development of the 'modernisation' agenda, and subsequent policy and legislation to support its implementation, the government's focus has been upon developing 'personalised' provision in adult social care.

Two key papers have provided guidance on personalisation.

Our Health, Our Care, Our Say: A New Direction for Community Services *(DH, 2006)*

This White Paper built on the Green Paper Independence, Well-being and Choice *(DH, 2005) and outlined the radical and sustained shift in the way services are delivered. Emphasis was given to developing individualised budgets for service users to develop personalised care pathways for excluded groups by increasing direct payments and the introduction of individualised budgets.*

Putting People First: A Shared Vision and Commitment to the Transformation of Adult Social Care *(DH, 2007b)*

This protocol set out the government's commitment to independent living for all adults. It also outlined the shared values and aims that the government suggests will guide the transformation of adult social care. It seeks to develop a collaborative approach between local and central government, the sector's professional leadership, providers and regulators to develop a personalised adult social care system.

The key elements of such a system were outlined as:

* *local authority leadership with genuine partnership working with local NHS, other statutory agencies, third and private sector providers, users and carers and the wider local community;*

agreed and shared outcomes, irrespective of illness or disability, for individuals to:

* *live independently;*

* *stay healthy;*

* *have maximum control over their life;*

* *sustain a family unit;*

* *participate as equal and active citizens, both economically and socially;*

* *have the best quality of life;*

* *retain maximum dignity and respect.*

Person-centred planning and self-directed support are to be the mainstream with personal budgets for everyone eligible for publicly funded adult social care support and family members and carers to be treated as care partners. The government suggested there is a need to explore long-term funding of care to ensure the system is fair, sustainable and unambiguous about respective responsibilities of the state, family and individual.

The role of personalisation as a cornerstone of modernisation in health and social care was heralded in the Department of Health's Green Paper *Independence, Well-being and Choice* (DH, 2005), followed by *Our Health, Our Care, Our Say: A New Direction for Community Services* (2006) and *Putting People First* (2007b). The focus of policy has been on how personalisation can improve health and social care provision through improving standards and changing structures of assessment and service development by utilising users of services' skills and knowledge to develop their own personalised services, a 'bottom–up' rather than 'top–down' approach (Leadbeater, 2004; Leadbeater et al., 2008).

Leadbeater et al. (2008) suggest improving provision for users of services is dependent on building the capacity of individuals to develop and manage self-directed health and social care pathways that transfer patterns of provision from the professional to the personal realm. This has been facilitated by government in the development of specific legislation, and approaches in social work that professionals are expected to use to promote personalisation; for example, individual budgets, direct payments and person-centred planning (Manthorpe et al., 2008). These measures support the government's strategy to break down the demarcation between professionals and non-professionals in restructuring health and social care provision (National School of Government, 2007). Ferguson (2004) suggests this is not a new strategy but rather a continuation of a process where the non-involvement of social workers in major social programmes is normal; for example, Sure Start and Supporting People.

Transformation

Government clearly identifies that further modernisation of social care through personalisation will require a massive cultural shift within organisations based on a transformational change at all levels and with all participants across the sector (DH, 2008a, p5).

Transforming Social Care LAC (DH) (2008a) 1

This circular sets out to support the previous White Papers Independence, Well-being and Choice *(DH, 2005),* Our Health, Our Care, Our Say *(DH, 2006) and* Putting People First *(DH, 2007b) and provides guidance on the next steps on the road to the transformation of social care.*

Part 1: Outlines the vision for the development of a personalised approach to the delivery of adult social care and suggests

> *The role of social workers will be focused on advocacy and brokerage, rather than assessment and gate keeping. (p4)*

Part 2: Outlines how social service departments will be supported to deliver this part of the modernisation agenda, suggesting

> *Personalisation is about whole system change. (p5)*

Whole-system change will be achieved by local engagement supported through:

- *public service agreements;*
- *local government National Indicator Set;*
- *local area agreements;*
- *strategic leadership across councils.*

At a national level, the Association of Directors and Social Services, Local Government Association and the Improvement and Development Agency will work together as a sector-led 'consortium' to support the transformation agenda.

At a regional level, Joint Improvement Partnerships will work with the Regional Improvement and Efficiency Partnerships to facilitate regional implementation and local activity, and provide local leadership.

These will support the goals of the National Improvement and Efficiency Strategy where:

- *social and health care will be measured against the National Indicator Set;*

- *this will inform the joint performance assessment undertaken by the Care Quality Commission and the Comprehensive Area Assessment.*

The reform of services has been welcomed by many in the profession. Change is accepted as a constant companion in social work yet there are concerns that these have also left many in the profession feeling marginalised, as a chasm appears to be developing between the rhetoric of policy and its implementation in practice, leaving some practitioners demotivated and disillusioned.

ACTIVITY 6.2

Team discussion

Read the comment below.

> *Being a care manager is very different from being a social worker as I had always thought of it. Care management is all about budgets and paperwork and the financial implications for the authority, whereas social work is about people. That's the crucial difference. (Jones, 2001, p553)*

Discuss with colleagues:

- *Does the above statement reflect your thoughts on social work and care management?*

- *What have 'modernisation', 'personalisation' and 'transformation' meant for you as a practitioner?*

- *Read the Jones (2001) article in full. Are these 'voices from the front line' representative of your voice?*

The impact of reform on practitioners

Research suggests that the modernisation agenda has had a detrimental effect on the social work workforce and led to disillusionment within the profession. Jones (2001) found social workers employed in the statutory sector suggested their biggest source of stress came from working within local and national policy and guidelines, while Huxley et al.'s (2005) survey of UK social workers in mental health found 28 per cent wanted to leave their posts and 21 per cent planned to. The study also acknowledged 'high levels of dissatisfaction with the job (53%) and employers (78%)' (p1072). Horner and Jones (2004) identified that push factors, such as feelings of frustration, outweighed pull factors, such as wage increases, in determining if social workers stayed in the public sector (Galpin, 2009). Stanley et al.'s (2007) study of depression in the workforce found that individuals perceived work as a strong factor in developing mental health difficulties, with nearly a quarter identifying the work environment as a key factor, especially in terms of the perceived constant change.

Factors that motivate practitioners to stay in the profession include high intrinsic levels of job satisfaction (Cameron, 2003), along with meaningful contact with service users (Huxley et al., 2005). Personalisation should, in theory, provide a route along which practitioners can engage meaningfully, with its emphasis on person-centred planning and focus on service users and carers' abilities to develop and manage self-directed care pathways. Manthorpe et al. (2008) suggest the 'process of personalisation will inevitably alter the world of social work and care management with adults' (p3). An assumption may be that this alteration will be positive for practitioners; however, has personalisation motivated the profession or has it only added to the current levels of disillusionment identified in research?

Concerns are already beginning to surface as government and employers appear to be of the opinion that disillusionment within the profession around personalisation is attributed to workers struggling with the loss of power as the client gains control over their services (Stapleton, 2008). Arguably, the problem is not loss of power but the loss of a critical professional voice that is listened to. Anecdotal evidence from post-qualifying social work students over the past 18 months has identified schemes such as direct payments and individual budgets as inappropriate for some older people. Practitioners have felt their concerns have been dismissed by government and employer; however, recent research supports their practice experience. Older people in receipt of individual budgets were found to experience lower psychological well-being than those who were not in receipt of an individual budget (Glendinning et al., 2008).

Research summary

Ferguson (2007) suggests the concept of personalisation occupies a central position in social work with adults today. However, its development has been driven not by social work but by the government think tank, Demos, and, in particular, Charles Leadbeater, 'a journalist and writer who has spent ten years working for the Financial Times *and is also an adviser to a number of major private companies, including Chanel Four Television and British Telecom (Leadbeater, 2006)' (p398). This has resulted in a 'flawed conception of the people who use services' (p400). Ferguson (2007) argues social workers should not accept personalisation uncritically, suggesting they should challenge it as a philosophy on which services are developed to ensure their practice takes into consideration structural issues that impact negatively on individuals. Otherwise practice may be oppressive when problems and solutions are located with the individual, and responsibility is transferred wholly from the state to the individual.*

Arguably, a gap is developing between practitioner and employer in the implementation of MPT which is fuelling disillusionment in the profession. Central government clearly identifies that successful transformation will only occur if front-line staff are engaged in the process (DH, 2008b); therefore, the gap has to be bridged. To achieve this, however, we might first consider under what conditions it has developed by exploring three interrelated factors:

- the use of language and ambiguity in meaning;
- the process of depoliticisation;
- leadership and management.

An exploration of the ambiguity in meaning of language used in social care today, along with the process of depoliticisation, can provide a useful insight into understanding how policy and practice interact and the role leadership and management has in the organisation and delivery of adult social care.

Language and ambiguity in meaning

Research summary: understanding language

Discourse is a key theme in social theory and draws on the works of French theorist Michel Foucault. Foucault makes clear links between discourse and power. Abercombie et al. (1994) define discourse as 'a domain of language use that is unified by common assumptions'.

Thompson (2003) suggests discourse is a 'way of talking and thinking' (p24) about aspects of life and is closely focused on language. Fook (2002) argues discourse is the way in which we make meaning of and construct our world through the language we use, verbal and non-verbal, to communicate about it. Fook (2002) suggests language is not neutral. Our language will be an expression of a particular attempt to make, or impose, meaning in a situation. Language is also about power. The language we use is an indication of which value systems or which groups are dominant in society.

Dichotomous thinking

Language and discourse maintains 'dichotomous thinking'. Dichotomous thinking implies that most phenomena fit into binary oppositional categories, in which one item in the binary is devalued in relation to the other, and mutually exclusive, that is, individual budgets versus local authority-arranged services.

Binary opposites

The way we represent our professional 'reality' through language is based on the tendency to order our world (make meaning) by categorising phenomena into 'binary opposites'. These are oppositional and hierarchical, and not seen as interdependent.

The categories we create have only two subsets which are mutually exclusive of each other, cast in opposing terms, with only one set valued over the other and not believed to be dependent on each other for definition. For example:

- *public sector vs private sector;*

- *professional vs non-professional;*

- *personalisation vs statutory services.*

The use of binary opposites is problematic. Binary opposites do not allow for a wealth of diverse meanings, experiences and identities to be represented in our discourses. Instead, the experience of the marginalised is often 'lumped together' in relation to the main-stream, thus perpetuating dominant discourses. For example, personalisation via individual budgets and direct payments is 'good' for all service users and statutory provi-sion is 'bad'. In this process, marginal individuals, such as those who are unable or unwilling to engage in direct payments and individual budget schemes, may be 'othered' or even silenced or ignored in relation to mainstream experience.

Direction from central government contained in policy and legislation frequently appears congruent with practitioners' social work values. Personalisation is a case in point. Ferguson (2007), however, suggests that personalisation is also an ambiguous term that exists alongside other congruent terms such as 'rights', 'risks', 'independence', 'well-being' and 'choice'. Ambiguity in meaning has led to an initial acceptance of the MPT agenda by many practitioners as social work professionals have assumed government, employers and users of services have a shared understanding of their meaning.

Ferguson (2007) and Carey (2009) suggest terminology is important to ensure its appeal to all audiences; for example, the notion of a 'bottom–up' approach will appeal to social workers as it appears consistent with their professional values and notions of human rights and empowerment. Some commentators suggest personalisation is an approach that has grown from the grass roots of service user and carer groups to promote service user and carer participation in the assessment, development and delivery of social care (Mansell and Beadle-Brown, 2004), while others suggest its roots are located in a neo-liberal free market approach to care provision (Ferguson, 2007) and that 'personalisation did not emerge from within social work or service users but from Demos, the New Labour think-tank. Another offshoot of consumerism, it draws on Thatcherite community care reforms and care management' (Rogowski, 2009, p27). The reality is that all these com-mentators are right to some extent; possibly the difficulty for practitioners has been an initial lack of awareness of the ideology and values that are driving implementation within organisational contexts. Uncritical acceptance of language can obscure more than it reveals if the ideology underpinning its usage is not identified. Ife (2008) suggests lan-guage and power are inextricably linked, stating 'language helps to define and reinforce power relationships, and that it is necessary to subject social work language to critical analysis if social workers are to be consistent in human rights practice' (p194).

'Choice' has been a prominent buzz word for MPT. Clarke (2005) suggests that choice is the engine of public sector reform, with choice seen as desirable in empowering individu-als to move from passive consumers to activated and responsibilised citizens. Choice as a concept remains controversial for some as it is also viewed as a route along which the marketisation of public services can travel without challenge (Clarke, 2005). Ferguson (2007) argues that while this is a logical extension of the modernisation agenda for government and those who support personalisation, for many a market approach to service delivery underpins the problems experienced in social work practice over the last 20 years.

Butler and Drakeford (2001) suggest that government has exploited this ambiguity to enable 'social workers to retain the semblance of loyalty to its own values, while carrying out the bidding of political masters with very different ideas and purposes' (p8, cited in Ferguson, 2007, p389). Arguably, organisational strategies have sought to build on ambiguity in meaning to 'manufacture consent' for the transformation of adult social care.

Courpasson and Dany (2001) explore how organisations manufacture consent and Courpasson (2000) introduces the notion that soft coercion induces, simultaneously, commitment and obedience to the organisation and its aims. Ambiguity in meaning may be one such instrument of soft coercion. Clearly, any act of coercion requires the exercise of power and control. Hall (1972) suggests that coercion is achieved by getting others to accept your perspective. To do this, credibility in the eyes of others is crucial. One strategy used to maintain obedience to organisational policies and obtain credibility has been the 'company song' (Parker, 1997), which, in the context of this argument, could be any number of words included in government policy whose meanings are nebulous to say the least; for example, 'independence' and 'well-being'. These appear consistent with social work values and help normalise organisational aims, making them unquestioningly acceptable to practitioners as a goal for practice, but what do they mean, and more importantly, what ideological perspective underpins their usage?

A second strategy used to maintain obedience is the use of rules. Clegg (1989) suggests rules are crucial in maintaining control in an organisation. Rules are part of the structure underpinning organisational life, they can also be 'fragile, ambiguous, unclear, and dependent upon interpretation' (Clegg 1989, p209). Organisations can take an authoritative approach to determining what the rules mean (Courpasson and Dany, 2001) and steer an individual towards a particular choice.

Again, anecdotal evidence from post-qualifying social work students suggests an authoritative rule-based approach to choice is common in practice today. 'Funding panels', for example, function as a mechanism to allocate resources. These allow managers to circumvent social workers' assessments to reshape 'choice'. Practitioners have suggested that panels frequently refuse funding applications from social workers for residential placements for older people, while requests for direct payments are not referred to panel and authorised unquestioningly. Reasons for this are speculative; however, performance indicators encourage local authorities to increase the uptake of direct payments and reduce the number of residential placements. This may provide panel members with an alternative company song; for example 'meeting performance indicators improves our star rating'. Evidence from CSCI (2008) would seem to support practitioners' experiences when they highlight a 100 per cent increase in spending on direct payments and a fall of 9 per cent in permanent residents supported by councils in care homes. Munro (2004) argues that anecdotal evidence suggests performance 'indicators are having a perverse effect on practice, with a concern for meeting government targets overriding a concern for the welfare of users' (p1086). This is borne out in more recent conversations with practitioners who suggest that in some areas of practice they only offer individual budgets to their service users, and 'choice' occurs only after this process. Therefore choice in service provision is conditional on acceptance of an individual budget. Since under the new performance framework, the National Indicator Set (DfCaLG, 2008), an increased uptake in individual budgets is an indicator of transformational success for local authorities, Munro's (2004) observation may still hold true. In this context, an authoritarian approach is able to manufacture consent for the extension of personalised services based on coercion rather than evidence of its efficacy.

ACTIVITY **6.3**

Team discussion

- *Can you identify areas in your practice where ambiguity in meaning, rules and/or 'soft coercion' has influenced your practice?*

- *How did this make you feel?*

- *How do you manage this?*

Depoliticisation and social care

ACTIVITY **6.4**

Collins (2009) asks 'Is "political involvement" part of the social work task? Is it part of the "job" or a function that is undertaken outside social work?' (p348)

- *How would you answer these questions?*

- *Does the organisational context of practice support your answers or act as a barrier to your answers?*

- *Does your answer make any difference to the individuals you work with?*

While a coercive approach may allow the public sector to provide personalised services that are 'better value for tax payers' money' (Leadbeater et al., 2008), MPT also provides a process whereby the relationship between individual and state is depoliticised, leading to a greater emphasis on a culture of blame if individuals fail to take responsibility for themselves. Burnham (2001) defines depoliticisation as the process of 'placing at one remove the political character of decision-making' (p127). As a governing strategy it enables government to have arms' length control of key economic and social processes while 'simultaneously benefiting from the distancing effects of depoliticisation' (p127). Buller and Flinders (2005) identify two benefits of such a strategy. First, devolving responsibility for policy-making to 'neutral, independent experts can be a way of enhancing the authority of political institutions' (p526). Second, 'depoliticisation can help to insulate politicians in office from the adverse consequences of policy failure' (p526). Burnham (2001) suggests depoliticisation is not the absence of the political from social and economic conditions or the removal of 'political power and influence' (p136), but rather a 'governing strategy' (p136) that is still very political. While personalisation is presented as a non-political 'bottom–up' approach to reforming health and social care (Leadbeater et al., 2008), is it really a top–down approach that seeks to transfer responsibility from government to non-government agencies and individuals based on neo-liberal ideology committed to the privatisation of public sector provision, based on free market principles (Taylor-Gooby and Lawson, 1993)?

Research into aspects of the personalisation agenda suggests such a process may actually decrease the psychological and emotional well-being of some users of services (Glendinning et al., 2008). This then leaves social work professionals struggling to work within a system that fails to recognise how some aspects of personalisation might not be appropriate in some areas of practice or accept how structural inequalities might impact on individual users of services (Carey, 2009). Personalisation is arguably as concerned with managing scarce resources (Le Grand et al., 2008) and 'getting more value for public money' (Leadbeater et al, 2008, p1) as improving emotional and psychological well-being (Glendinning et al, 2008). This is not to suggest these concerns are incompatible but rather that there may be an incongruence between government and professional beliefs about the purpose of personalisation and that this has led to growing disillusionment within the social work workforce.

Burnham (2001) suggests the public sector now consists of a set of permeable relationships between the public and private sectors in the provision of services, along with a mix of responsibilities. While it might allow greater participation of service users and carers in the development and delivery of care services, government has also developed a number of regulatory requirements that need to be met. This, Cope and Goodship (1999) suggest, is used by government as a control mechanism, 'enhancing central government's management while off-loading difficult issues of provision' (cited in Burnham, 2001, p140). This may prove beneficial for some but it may also lead us into a culture of blame, where failure to support oneself is attributed to the individual, without considering how structural processes might increase discrimination and oppression. Carey (2009) suggests the language of service user and carer participation can act as 'a mirage that conceals very different agendas' (p181). Humphreys' (2004) exploration of immigration policy in Britain provides insight into the effect this can have on practitioners, suggesting that by 'not reflecting on structural and cultural levels of discrimination and oppression, practitioners deceive themselves that their practice is actually anti-discriminatory and anti-oppressive by adopting an individualistic approach' (p95).

Transformational and transactional leadership and management

While the language from central government speaks of transformation (DH, 2008a), one wonders how this approach will differ from modernisation when one considers that transformation appears to be centred around the same ambiguities of meaning and processes of depoliticisation, along with the same agencies and agreements, that has supported modernisation? As with modernisation, transformation involves at a national level the Association of Directors of Adult Social Services, the Local Government Association and the Improvement and Delivery Agency, who are expected to work with a sector-led 'consortium' to support the transformation agenda. Public Service Agreements and Local Area Agreements will support local input. At a regional level, Joint Improvement Partnerships and Regional Improvement and Efficiency Partnerships will work together to facilitate regional implementation and local activity. The success of transformation will be measured against a series of performance indicators; for example, the National Improvement and Efficiency Strategy (DfCaLG, 2008), which outlines the first of its four underpinning themes as 'improving value for money to meet the 3 per cent efficiency target' (p7).

With success measured against cost savings and performance indicators, will transformation be delivered using the same transactional leadership and management that appears to already dominate practice today and what effect might this have on the social work profession? Burns (1978) suggests transactional leadership is based on bureaucratic authority and legitimacy within the organisation. Transactional leaders emphasise 'work standards, assignments, and task orientated goals' (Eppard, 2004, p3). An organisation characterised by a transactional management structure may also lead to the development of a 'defensive culture' (Eppard, 2004) where members are expected to conform and follow rules without challenge. This describes some practitioners' experiences of practice today (Horner and Jones, 2004; Huxley et al., 2005).

However, Burns (1978) suggests that transformational leadership is a process that motivates followers by appealing to higher ideals and moral values. Transformational leaders must be able to define and articulate a vision for their organisations, and the followers must accept the credibility of the leader (Eppard, 2004, p3). Organisations characterised by transformational leadership are more likely to have a 'constructive culture' (Eppard, 2004) where members experience constructive cultural norms; for example, organisations set challenging but realistic goals and manage in a participative manner where relationships are constructive and open so as to achieve agreed goals (Cooke and Rousseau, 1988). Possibly a transformational approach could provide the impetus for the social work profession to fully engage in the transformation of social care and reduce current levels of disillusionment. However, this is not to suggest transactional leadership and management is not required. Think back to our discussion on 'binary opposites'. Eppard (2004) suggests both approaches are required in any large organisation. It might be that within social work settings the transactional approach has carried greater emphasis than the transformational, and that this has been, if not encouraged, at least supported by managerial approaches incorporated from the business sector. In this context the focus of practice is on regulation and targets, leading practitioners to manage those who use services 'rather than to work jointly with them to help them realise their rights' (Galpin and Parker, 2007, p9).

Critical commentary and reflection

Tsui and Cheung (2004) suggest 'managerialism' has become the dominant model of management in the public sector. They define managerialism as a 'set of beliefs and practices that assumes better management will resolve a wide range of economic and social problems' (p437) and summarise the ethos of managerialism in the human services in eight key points.

1 *The client is a customer (not a service consumer).*

2 *The manager (not front-line staff) is the key.*

3 *The staff are employees (not professionals).*

4 *Management knowledge (not common sense or professional knowledge) is the dominant model of knowledge in the development and delivery of services.*

5 *The market (not society or community) is the environment in which care is developed and provided.*

6 *Efficiency (not effectiveness) is the yardstick for measuring the performance of an organisation and its staff.*

7 *Cash and contracts (not care and concern) are the foundation of relationships.*

8 *Quality is equated with standardisation and documentation.*

Reflection

- *What is your experience of management within your workplace – is it transactional or transformational?*

- *Identify the pros and cons of managerialism.*

- *What changes would you make to management within your organisation to improve services to individuals and your experience as an employee?*

A human rights-based approach to MPT

ACTIVITY 6.5

Defining and understanding human rights is a contested and problematic area, and as such requires far more depth of analysis than can be provided in this chapter (see recommended reading at the end of the chapter); however, to develop a human rights-based approach to practice one must avoid 'ambiguity in meaning' and clarify what human rights are.

The Human Rights Act 1998 provides a framework for understanding what human rights are. However, what is a human rights-based approach to practice?

- *Write down our 'Human Rights' as defined in the Act.*

- *How are these linked to practice?*

- *What other frameworks support a human rights-based approach to practice?*

An inquiry by the Equality and Human Rights Commission (EHRC) suggests that where public sector providers embrace a human rights-based approach, they reported improved services along with 'better and more coherent delivery procedures and heightened staff morale' (2009, p21). Using an example from mental health services, the Commission identified the positive effect a human rights-based approach can have on service users, the quality of care and change in culture within an NHS trust (p21). The Commission states 'The Human Rights Act provides a common framework of values that can be useful for managing competing tensions and ethical obligations within a public authority and between professionals engaged in inter-agency work' (2009, p21).

Therefore, a human rights-based approach may provide a framework for practice activity that is able to address issues of ambiguity in meaning and depoliticisation and facilitate genuine transformation in adult social care while reducing disillusionment in some parts of the profession. However, the profession's relationship with human rights might first require some work. Healy (2008) suggests social work's visibility, in terms of the human rights movement, has been low, attributing this, in part, to its 'focus on needs rather than rights' (p744) and limited 'leadership on human rights by the organisations that represent the profession' (p745). It was envisaged that the introduction of the Human Rights Act 1998 would introduce a culture of human rights in statutory health and social care, with the key components of respect, equality and dignity as standard practice, and while there is evidence to suggest human rights have led to some improvements (EHRC, 2009), sadly, it would appear, this is not always the case.

A report from the Local Government Ombudsman (2009) into the deaths of six individuals with a learning disability in contact with health and social care professionals suggests 'despite the fact that ten years have elapsed since the introduction of the Human Rights Act 1998, our investigation . . . demonstrates that an underlying culture which values human rights was not in place' (p21). The report states that 'the lack of respect for these principles spread across many organisations. The absence of understanding of individual needs, empathy . . . and a basic concern for them as people led to prolonged suffering and inappropriate care' (p21).

Adherence to a culture of human rights has the ability to provide professional and organisational practice with a clear framework on which to hang the transformation of adult social care. To achieve this, the profession, and those in leadership in the organisations in which they work, may need to actively view their engagement with users of services as 'securing human rights for individuals' (Healy, 2008, p746) because 'what is missing, perhaps, is a consciousness of the activities of social work as human rights practice and of ways to build on individual case solutions to influence policy change' (p746).

Government has made it clear in the context of health and social care that the role of the social worker will be different, not lesser (DH, 2007b). While that role is not clearly defined, new roles such as Best Interest Assessor under the Mental Capacity Act (2005) and Deprivation of Liberty Safeguards are developing and call on practitioners to take a lead role in decision-making to address breaches of Article 5 of the Human Rights Act 1998. Although the foundations of this legislation are firmly embedded in the protection of individuals' human rights, Ife (2008) warns social workers 'that to "act in the best interests of" another person can easily become itself a human rights violation, and that such social work must be undertaken only with a sense of deep unease and moral questioning' (p173). The requirement for practitioners to frame their practice in a human rights approach is further supported by the EHRC (2009) findings on the extent to which human rights is embedded in public sector practice. It suggests 'vulnerable and excluded groups within society were less likely to know their rights and less likely to have the capacity and/or confidence to assert their rights' (p11) and therefore require support to ensure their human rights are not breached. This may indicate the change of role central government envisages, one that may enable the profession to reassert its professional voice as practitioners refocus on rights rather than needs. While 'assessment of need' is viewed as at the core of social work practice, and in this sense unproblematic, need is actually a subjective concept, and assessment of need in social work practice will be influenced by a number of factors, such as individual practitioners' values and beliefs, organisational priorities and the requirements of policy and legislation. Ife (2008) states 'Rights-based practice is a form of social work where the word "right" is used more than the word "need" in the day-to-day discourse of social workers' (p94). This is central to a human rights-based approach to practice. However, to achieve this will require the type of transformational leadership spoken of above – a form of leadership that develops and engages with professionals to transform organisational cultures built on the value of individuals' human rights, as well as providing value for money. The two are not incompatible, but may require some truly transformational thinking, and action, from both practitioners and leaders, to reform adult social care.

The EHRC (2009) have identified that lack of leadership from those in power within organisations such as the NHS and Social Care, along with central government and some politicians, act as a major barrier to developing a human rights-based framework within the public sector, recommending 'those with leadership roles should recognise their responsibility to provide a robust leadership on human rights issues' (p10). For practitioners, the need to actively ensure they understand and engage in the promotion of human rights is made clear by the EHRC (2009) when it suggests that within the public sector workforce there 'is insufficient understanding that human rights can be a tool for improving peoples lives' (p11).

Research summary and reflection

The Equality and Human Rights Commission conducted an inquiry to establish the extent to which human rights are embedded in service provision across England and Wales in the public sector. There were 2,855 individuals who provided evidence to the inquiry between April and December 2008. The aim of the inquiry was to identify barriers to the delivery of human rights and identify good practice to support the promotion of human rights.

The report from the inquiry identified everyday situations in which the Human Rights Act might apply: some that practitioners may encounter are listed below.

- *Not being able to eat properly while in hospital or a care home (Articles 2 and 8).*

- *Provision of facilities or food which do not meet religious or cultural needs (Article 9).*

- *Abuse or neglect of older people, those who are learning disabled or other vulnerable people (Articles 2 and 3).*
- *Lack of respect for privacy on a hospital ward (Article 8).*
- *Not respecting gay and lesbian partners as next of kin or inheritors of tenancies (Articles 8 and 14).*
- *Excessive surveillance of law-abiding people (Article 8).*
- *Loss of personal data by public officials (Article 8).*
- *Failure by authorities to protect people from being stalked and harassed (Articles 2, 3 and 8).*
- *Not being sufficiently protected from domestic violence (Articles 2, 3 and 8).*
- *Not being allocated suitable housing for special needs that have been identified (Article 8).*
- *Unexplained death in prisons, police stations and psychiatric hospitals (Article 2).*

Reflection

- *Have you encountered any circumstances where the situation might constitute a breach of an individual's human rights?*
- *How did you resolve this situation?*
- *What would you do in the future?*

Developing a human rights-based approach to practice

The social work profession should be thriving as MPT focuses on users of services taking centre stage with increased control over the services they receive – the embodiment of empowerment. Research would seem to suggest some social work practitioners are disillusioned with the current context of practice (Jones, 2001; Horner and Jones, 2004; Huxley et al., 2005; Stanley et al., 2007) as social work professionals are experiencing ever-increasing levels of stress and changes have left 'many feeling demoralised and devalued' (McDonald et al., 2008, p3). Ambiguity in meaning and a process of depoliticisation has meant that, for some, the implementation of MPT is incongruent with core social work values (Ferguson, 2007), paying limited attention to structural issues, such as poverty and inequality (Ferguson, 2007). Arguably, just as Gorman and Postle (2003) identified practitioners' awareness of the rhetoric of community care and the reality of everyday practice, social workers are finding a gap that exists between their professional values and the organisational context of practice.

However, there is an adequate framework in the shape of the human rights available to organisational leaders and practitioners to ensure their leadership and practice is transformative. This may then motivate and re-engage the social work profession to contribute meaningfully to reform. However, the profession may first need to find ways of ensuring its critical professional voice is heard.

Government frequently addresses social problems using buzzwords such as 'knife crime', 'alcohol abuse' or 'a gang culture'. However, practitioners are aware that these 'problems' are also associated with 'structural forces to do with inequality, perceived lack of opportunity . . . and so on' (Ife, 2008, p210) where no end of restructuring of social care provision at an individual or cultural level is able to address what are, effectively, structural issues.

Within this process of change, practitioners are presented with opportunities. Ife (2008) states 'social work is constantly being redefined . . . it is important for human rights-based social workers to become part of that redefinition and actively engage in the processes of re-structuring, so that structures more conducive to the realisation of human rights can be facilitated' (p210).

Defining a human rights-based approach to practice

The Human Rights Act 1998 provides a legal framework for understanding human rights; however, one might combine this with professional codes of practice to construct a framework to support a human rights-based approach to social work practice. Cemlyn (2008) provides further guidance on linkage between human rights and codes of ethics identifying the international and national codes of ethics that support professional practice.

The code from the International Federation of Social Workers (2001) suggests social work is:

> *A profession which promotes social change, problem solving in human relationships and the empowerment and liberation of people to enhance well-being. Utilising theories of human behaviour and social systems, social work intervenes at the points where people interact with their environments. Principles of human rights and social justice are fundamental to social work.*

Cemlyn (2008) suggests the British code 'spells out that this means upholding not only civil and political but also economic, social and cultural rights' (p156), concluding 'the pursuit of social justice involves identifying, seeking to alleviate and advocating strategies for overcoming structural disadvantage'.

One might argue that a human rights-based approach to practice is politically and socially aware, actively advocates against the oppression of those who use services and engages with those who use services and other professionals to challenge discrimination at a cultural, structural and personal level.

Reflection

- *How would you define human rights-based practice?*
- *How could you use this to develop your practice?*
- *How could this be used in leadership and management?*

Chapter summary

- The organisation and delivery of health and social care has undergone significant change.

- Social work practitioners have struggled in some areas of practice with change leading to feelings of dissatisfaction.

- A misunderstanding between the rhetoric of policy and reality of practice threatens to derail the transformation of adult social care.

- Leadership and management have an important role in engaging practitioners in the transformation agenda.

- A human rights-based approach to practice could provide a unifying strategy to achieve transformative services and organisational structures.

- Social work practitioners need to actively engage in understanding the political context of practice to ensure their critical professional voice is heard.

FURTHER READING

Healy, L.M. (2008) Exploring the history of social work as a human rights profession. *International Social Work,* 51(6): 735–748.

Ife, J. (2008) *Human rights and social work: towards rights-based practice.* Melbourne: Cambridge University Press.

References

Abercrombie, N., Turner, B.S. and Hill, S. (1994) *The Penguin dictionary of sociology*. London: Penguin.

Adams, R. (2002) *Social policy for social work*. Hampshire: Palgrave Macmillan.

Adams, R. (2005) Working within and across boundaries: tensions and dilemmas. In R. Adams, L. Dominelli and M. Payne (eds), *Social work futures crossing boundaries: transforming practice*. Hampshire: Palgrave Macmillan.

Adams, R., Dominelli, L. and Payne, M. (eds) (2002) *Social work: themes, issues and critical debates*. Basingstoke: Palgrave Macmillan.

Ahmed, W.I.U (2000) *Ethnicity, disability and chronic illness*. Buckingham: Open University Press.

Alcock, P., Erskine, A. and May, M. (1999) *The student's companion to social policy*. Oxford: Blackwell.

Askheim, O.P. (2005) Personal assistance – direct payments or alternative public service. Does it matter for the promotion of user control? *Disability and Society*, 20(3): 247–60.

Association of Directors of Social Services (2005) *Safeguarding adults*. London: The Association of Directors of Social Services.

Banks, S. (2006) *Ethics and values in social work*. Basingstoke: Palgrave Macmillan.

Barnett, M. (2006) Social constructivism. In J. Baylis and S. Smith (eds), *Globalisation of world politics*. Oxford: Oxford University Press.

Bates, P. and Davis, F. (2004) Social capital, social inclusion and services for people with learning disabilities. *Disability and Society*, 19(3): 195–207.

Bauld, L., Chesterman, J., Davies, B., Judge, K. and Mangalore, R. (2000) *Caring for older people: an assessment of community care in the 1990s*. Aldershot: Ashgate.

Beckett, C. and Maynard, A. (2005) *Values and ethics in social work*. London: Sage.

Benjamin, A. (2008) Breaking the mould. *The Guardian*, Society section, 11 June.

Beresford, P. (2005) Redistributing profit and loss: the new economics of the market and social welfare. *Critical Social Policy*, 25(4): 464–82.

Biggs, S. (1993) *Understanding ageing*. Oxford: Open University Press.

Biggs, S., Phillipson, C., Money, A. and Leach, R. (2008) The age-shift: observations on social policy, ageism and the dynamics of the adult life course. *Journal of Social Work Practice*, 20(3): 239–50.

Billig, M. (2001) Discursive, rhetorical and ideological messages. In M. Wetherell, S. Taylor and S.J. Yates (eds) *Discourse theory and practice: a reader*. London: Sage.

Bowers, H., Bailey, B., Sanderson, H., Easterbrook, L. and Macadam, A. (2007) *Person centred thinking with older people: practicalities and possibilities*. Cheshire: HSA Press.

Braye, S. and Preston-Shoot. M. (1995) *Empowering practice in social care.* Buckingham: Open University Press.

Brechin, A., Brown, H. and Eby, M.A. (2000) *Critical practice in health and social care.* London: Sage.

British Association of Social Workers (2002) *Code of ethics for social workers.* Birmingham: BASW.

British Institute of Human Rights (2008) *Health and Social Care Bill: House of Lords, Committee Briefing.* Online: **www.bihr.org.uk/sites/default/files/HealthAndSocialCareBill_briefing2.pdf** (accessed 1 July 2009).

Brown, K. (2006) *Vulnerable adults and community care.* Exeter: Learning Matters.

Brown, R. and Barber, P. (2008) *The social worker's guide to the Mental Capacity Act 2005.* Exeter: Learning Matters.

Buller, J. and Flinders, M. (2005) The domestic origins of depoliticisation in the area of British economic policy. *British Journal of Politics and International Relations,* 7: 526–43.

Burnham, P. (2001) New Labour and the politics of depoliticisation. *British Journal of Politics and International Relations,* 3(2): 127–49.

Burns, J. M. (1978) *Leadership.* New York: Harper Row.

Cambridge, P. (1999) Building care management competence in services for people with learning disabilities. *British Journal of Social Work,* 29: 393–415.

Cambridge, P. and Carnaby, S. (2005) *Person centred planning and care management with people with learning disabilities.* London: Jessica Kingsley.

Cameron, C. (2003) Care work and care workers. In Social Care Workforce Research Unit, *Social care workforce research: needs and priorities.* London: King's College London.

Carers and Disabled Children Act 2000. (c.16). London: HMSO.

Carers (Equal Opportunities) Act 2004. (c.15). London: HMSO.

Carers (Recognition and Services) Act 1995. (c.12). London: HMSO.

Carers UK (2008) *The case for change: why England needs a new care and support system.* London: Carers UK. Online: **www.carersuk.org/Newsandcampaigns/Parliamentary/Responsesto government/Careandsupportconsultation.pdf** (accessed 1 July 2009).

Carers UK (2009) Policy briefing: *Facts about carers.* London: Carers UK. Online: **www.carersuk.org/Professionals/ResourcesandBriefings/Policybriefings/FactsaboutcarersJune200 9.pdf** (accessed 1 July 2009).

Carey, M. (2009) Critical commentary: happy shopper? The problem with service user and carer participation. *British Journal of Social Work,* 39(1): 179–88.

Carmichael, A. and Brown, L. (2002) The future challenge for direct payments. *Disability and Society,* 17(7): 797–808.

Carr, S. (2007) Participation, power, conflict and change: theorizing dynamics of service user participation in the social care system of England and Wales. *Critical Social Policy,* 27(2): 266–76.

Carr, S. and Robbins, D. (2009) *The implementation of individual budget schemes in adult social care.* London: SCIE.

Carson, D. and Bain, A. (2008) *Professional risk and working with people.* London: Jessica Kingsley.

Cartwright, R. (2009) Social workers 'too expensive' for personalisation. *Professional Social Work: BASW*, March: 5.

Cemlyn, S. (2008) Human rights and gypsies and travellers: an exploration of the application of a human rights perspective to social work with a minority community in Britain. *British Journal of Social Work*, 38: 153–73.

Clark, C. (1998) Self-determination and paternalism in community care: practice and prospects, *British Journal of Social Work,* 28: 387–402.

Clark, H. (2006) 'Its meant that, well, I'm living a life now'. Older people's experience of direct payments. In J. Leece and J. Bornat (eds), *Developments in direct payments.* Bristol: Policy Press.

Clark, H., Gough, H. and Macfarlane, A. (2004a) *'It pays dividends'. Direct payments and older people.* Bristol: The Policy Press.

Clark, H., Gough, H. and Macfarlane, A. (2004b) *Making direct payments work for older people.* Bristol: The Policy Press. Online: **www.jrf.org.uk/publications/making-direct-payments-work-older-people** (accessed 2 July 2009).

Clarke, J. (2001) Globalization and welfare states: some unsettling thoughts. In R. Sykes, B. Palier and P. Prior (eds), *Globalization and European welfare states.* Basingstoke: Palgrave.

Clarke, J. (2005) New Labour's citizens: activated, empowered, responsibilized, abandoned? *Critical Social Policy,* 25(4): 447–63.

Clegg, S. (1989) *Frameworks of power.* London: Sage.

Clements, L. (2000) *Community care and the law.* 2nd edn. London: Legal Action Group.

Clements, L. (2007) *Carers and their rights. The law relating to carers.* 2nd edn. London: Carers UK.

Clements, L. (2008a) *Individual budgets and carers (pre-publication draft paper).* Online: **www.luke-clements.co.uk/whatsnew/index.php** (accessed 1 July 2009).

Clements, L. (2008b) *Individual budgets and irrational exuberance (pre-publication paper).* Available from: **http://www.lukeclements.co.uk/whatsnew/index.php** (accessed 2 July 2009).

Clements, J. and Martin, N. (2002) *Assessing behaviours regarded as problematic for people with developmental disabilities.* London: Jessica Kingsley.

Collins, S. (2009) Some critical perspectives on social work and collectives. *British Journal of Social Work*, 39(2): 334–52.

Commission for Social Care Inspection (2004a) *Direct payments: what are the barriers?* London: CSCI.

Commission for Social Care Inspection (2004b) *When I get older: what people want from social care services and inspections, as they get older.* London: CSCI.

Commission for Social Care Inspection (2006) *Making choices: taking risks. A discussion paper.* London: CSCI.

Commission for Social Care Inspection (2008) *The state of social care in England 2006–07*. London: CSCI.

Commission for Social Care Inspection (2009) *The state of social care in England* 2007/08. London: CSCI.

Community Care (2008) New equality laws to leave services with massive bill. *Community Care,* 3 July: 9.

Community Care (2009) Directors reject BASW's 'scaremongering' over job fears. *Community Care,* 26 March: 5.

Cooke, R.A. and Rousseau, D.M. (1988) Behavioural norms and expectations. *Group and Organisational Studies,* 13(3): 245–73.

Cope, S. and Goodship, J. (1999) Regulating collaborative government. *Public Policy and Administration,* 14(2): 3–12.

Courpasson, D. (2000) Managerial domination and power in soft bureaucracy. *Organisation Studies,* 21(1): 141–61.

Courpasson, D. and Dany, F. (2001) The organisation of obedience soft coercion and strategies of subordination in business firms. *Organisation Studies (Special Issue),* 9: 1–26.

Croft, S. and Beresford, P. (1996) The politics of participation. In D. Taylor (ed), *Critical Social Policy: A Reader*. London: Sage.

Daily Mail (2007) Killer of headteacher still poses 'a genuine and present risk'. *Daily Mail,* 21 July. Online: **www.dailymail.co.uk/news/article-476572/Killer-headteacher-poses-genuine-present-risk.html** (accessed 1 July 2009).

Davey, V., Fernandez J.L., Knapp, M., Vick, N., Jolly, D., Swift, P., Tobin, R., Kendall, J., Ferrie, J., Pearson, C. and Mercer, G. (2007) *Direct payments: a national survey of direct payments policy and practice*. London: PSSRU, London School of Economics.

Davies, C., Finlay, L. and Bullman, A. (2000) *Changing practice in health and social care*. London: Open University Press.

Davies, M. (1999) *The Blackwell companion to social work*. Oxford: Blackwell.

Department for Communities and Local Government (2008) *National improvement and efficiency strategy*. London: TSO.

Department of Health (1989) *Caring for people: community care in the next decade and beyond*. London: HMSO.

Department of Health (1997) *The new NHS*. London: HMSO.

Department of Health (1998a) *Modernising social services*. London: HMSO.

Department of Health (1998b) *National priorities guidance*. London: HMSO.

Department of Health (1998c) *Modern local government: in touch with the people*. London: HMSO.

Department of Health (1999a) *Caring about carers: a national strategy for carers*. London: HMSO.

Department of Health (1999b) *Modernising government*. London: HMSO.

Department of Health (2000) *No secrets: guidance on developing and implementing multi-agency policies and procedures to protect vulnerable adults from abuse.* London: HMSO.

Department of Health (2001a) *National service framework for older people.* London: HMSO.

Department of Health (2001b) *Valuing people: a new strategy for learning disability for the 21st century.* London: HMSO.

Department of Health (2002) *Fair access to care services: guidance on eligibility criteria for adult social care.* London: HMSO.

Department of Health (2005) *Independence, well-being and choice: our vision for the future of social care for adults in England.* London: HMSO.

Department of Health (2006) *Our health, our care, our say: a new direction for community services.* London: HMSO.

Department of Health (2007a) *Independence, choice and risk: a guide to supported decision making.* London: HMSO.

Department of Health (2007b) *Putting people first: a shared vision and commitment to the transformation of adult social care.* London: HMSO.

Department of Health (2008a) *Transforming social care.* LAC (DH) (2008) 1. London: HMSO.

Department of Health (2008b) *Carers at the heart of 21st century families and communities.* London: HMSO.

Department of Health (2009) *Valuing people now.* London: HMSO.

Department of Health and Social Services Inspectorate (1991) *Care management and assessment practitioners guide.* London: HMSO.

Dominelli, L. (2002) Anti-oppressive practice in social work. In R. Adams, L. Dominelli and M. Payne (eds), *Social work: themes, issues and critical debates.* Basingstoke: Palgrave Macmillan.

Dominelli, L. (2004) *Social work: theory and practice for a changing profession.* Cambridge: Polity Press.

Ellis, K. (2007) Direct payments and social work practice: the significance of 'street level bureaucracy' in determining eligibility. *British Journal of Social Work,* 37: 405–22.

Emerson, E. and Stancliffe, R. (2004) Planning and action: comments on Mansell and Beadle-Brown. *Journal of Applied Research in Intellectual Disabilities,* 17: 23–6.

Equality and Human Rights Commission (2009) *Public perceptions of human rights. Human rights inquiry executive summary, report of the Equality and Human Rights Commission.* London: Equality and Human Rights Commission.

Eppard, R.G. (2004) *Transformational and transactional leadership styles as they predict constructive culture and defensive culture.* Virginia: Faculty of the Virginia Polytechnic Institute and State University.

Fenge, L. (2001) Empowerment and community care: projecting the 'voice' of older people. *Journal of Social Welfare and Family Law,* 23(4): 427–39.

Ferguson, I. (2004) Neoliberalism, the third way and social work: the UK experience. *Social Work and Society,* 2(1): 1–9.

Ferguson, I. (2007) Increasing user choice or privatising risk? The antinomies of personalisation. *British Journal of Social Work,* 37(3): 387–403.

Ferguson, I., Lavalette, M. and Whitmore, E. (eds) (2005) *Globalisation, global justice and social work.* Oxfordshire: Routledge.

Fine, M. and Glendinning, C. (2005) Dependence, independence or inter-dependence? Revisiting the concepts of 'care' and 'dependency'. *Ageing and Society,* 25: 601–21.

Fisher, B. and Tronto, J. (1990) Toward a feminist theory of caring. In E.K. Abel and M. Nelson (eds) *Circles of care.* Albany State: University of New York Press.

Flynn, M. (2006) Joint investigation into the provision of services for people with learning disabilities at Cornwall Partnership NHS Trust. *The Journal of Adult Protection,* 8(3): 28–32.

Fook. J. (2002) *Social work critical theory and practice.* London: Sage.

Foster, M., Harris, J., Jackson, K., Morgan, H. and Glendinning, C. (2006) Personalised social care for adults with disabilities: a problematic concept for frontline practice. *Health and Social Care in the Community,* 12(2): 125–35.

Galpin, D. (2009) Who really drives the development of post qualifying social work education and what are the implications of this? *Social Work Education,* 28(1): 65–80.

Galpin, D. and Parker, J.L. (2007) Adult protection in mental health and inpatient settings: an analysis of the recognition of adult abuse and use of adult protection procedures in working with vulnerable adults. *Journal of Adult Protection,* 9(2): 6–14.

General Social Care Council (2002) *Codes of practice for social care workers and employers.* London: GSCC.

Gilbert, P. (2006) *Social care services and the social perspective: learning about intellectual disabilities and health.* Online: **www.intellectualdisability.info/values/index.htm** (accessed 2 July 2009).

Glasby, J. and Littlechild, R. (2002) *Social work and direct payments.* Bristol: Policy Press.

Glendinning, C., Challis, D., Fernandez, J., Jacobs, S., Jones, K., Knapp, M., Manthorpe, J., Moran, N., Netten, A., Stevens, M. and Wilberforce, M. (2008) *Evaluation of the individual budgets pilot programme: final report.* York: Social Policy Research Unit, University of York.

Gorman, H. (2005) Frailty and dignity in old age. In R. Adams, L. Dominelli and M. Payne (eds), *Social work futures crossing boundaries, transforming practice.* Hampshire: Palgrave Macmillan.

Gorman, H. and Postle, K. (2003) *Transforming community care: a distorted vision?* Birmingham: Venture Press.

Grant, L. (1996) Effects of ageism on individual and health care providers' responses to healthy ageing. *Health and Social Work,* 21: 9–15.

Griffiths, R. (1988) *Community care: agenda for action.* London: HMSO.

Gross, R. (1996) *Psychology: the science of mind and behaviour.* London: Hodder and Stoughton.

Hagestad, G.O. and Uhlenberg, P. (2005) The social separation of old and young: a root of ageism. *Journal of Social Issues,* 61(2): 343–60.

Hall, P.M. (1972) A symbolic interactionist analysis of politics. *Sociological Inquiry,* 42: 35–75.

Harris, J. (2005) Globalisation, neo-liberal managerialism and UK social work. In I. Ferguson, M. Lavalette and E. Whitmore (eds), *Globalisation, global justice and social work.* Oxfordshire: Routledge.

Hasler, F. (2003) *Clarifying the evidence on direct payments into practice.* London: National Council for Independent Living.

Hasler, F., Zarb, G. and Campbell, J. (1998) *Key issues for local authority implementation of direct payments.* London: Policy Studies Institute.

Hatton, C., Waters, J., Duffy, S., Senker, J., Crosby, N., Poll, C., Tyson, A., O'Brien, J. and Towell, D. (2008) *A report on In Control's second phase 2005–7.* London: In Control.

Health and Social Care Act 2008. (c.14). London: HMSO.

Healy, K. (2005) *Social work theories in context: creating frameworks for practice.* Basingstoke: Palgrave Macmillan.

Healy, L.M. (2008) Exploring the history of social work as a human rights profession. *International Social Work,* 51(6): 735–48.

Henwood, M. and Hudson, B. (2008) Checking the FACS. *The Guardian,* 13 April.

Horner, L. and Jones, A. (2004) *Living on the frontline. A future for the civil service.* London: The Work Foundation.

Hudson, B. (2009) Captives of bureaucracy. *Community Care,* 9 April: 30–1.

Hudson, B. and Henwood, M. (2008) *Prevention, personalisation and prioritisation in social care: squaring the circle?* London: CSCI.

Hughes, B. (1995) *Older people and community care: critical theory and practice.* Buckingham: Open University Press.

Human Rights Act 1998. (c.42). London: HMSO.

Humphreys, B. (2004) An unacceptable role for social work: implementing immigration policy. *British Journal of Social Work,* 34: 93–107.

Hunter, M. (2007) Updating the 1999 carers' strategy. *Community Care,* 4 April. Online: **www. communitycare.co.uk/articles/2007/04/04/104061/updating-the-1999-carers-strategy.html** (accessed 25 August 2009).

Huxley, P., Evans, S., Gately, C., Webber, M., Mears, A., Pajak, S., Kendall, T., Medina J. and Katona C. (2005) Stress and pressures in mental health social work: the worker speaks. *British Journal of Social Work,* 35(7): 1063–79.

Ife, J. (2008) *Human rights and social work: towards rights-based practice.* Melbourne: Cambridge University Press.

International Federation of Social Work (2001) *Definition of social work.* Berne: International Federation of Social Work.

Johns, R. (2007) Who decides now? Protecting and empowering vulnerable adults who lose the capacity to make decisions for themselves. *British Journal of Social Work,* 37: 557–64.

Jones, C. (2001) Voices from the frontline: state social workers and New Labour. *British Journal of Social Work,* 31(4): 547–62.

Jones, C. (2005) The neo-liberal assault: voices from the front line of British state social work. In I. Ferguson, M. Lavalette and E. Whitmore (eds), *Globalisation, global justice and social work.* Abingdon: Routledge, pp95–108.

Jordan, B. with Jordan, C. (2000) *Social work and the third way: tough love as social policy.* 2nd edn. London: Sage.

Kemshall, H. (2002) *Risk, social policy and welfare.* Buckingham: Open University Press.

Leadbeater, C. (2004) *Personalisation through participation: a new script for public services.* London: Demos.

Leadbeater, C. and Miller, P. (2004) *The pro-am revolution: how enthusiasts are changing our society and economy.* London: Demos.

Leadbeater, C., Bartlett, B. and Gallagher, N. (2008) *Making it personal.* London: Demos.

Leece, J. (2003) The development of domiciliary care: what does the future hold? *Practice,* 15(3): 17–30.

Leece, J. (2004) Money talks, but what does it say? Direct payments and the commodification of care. *Practice,* 16(3): 211–21.

Leece, J. and Bornat, J. (2006) *Developments in direct payments.* Bristol: Policy Press.

Leece, D. and Leece, J. (2006) Direct payments: creating a two-tiered system in social care? *British Journal of Social Work,* 36: 1379–93.

Le Grand, J., Propper, C. and Smith, S. (2008) *The economics of social problems.* 4th edn. Basingstoke: Palgrave Macmillan.

Le Mesurier, N., Bathia, N. and Unwin. G.L. (2007) *Guide to services for young people with learning difficulties/disabilities and mental health problems/challenging behaviour: technical document: chapter 4.3 literature review – person centred planning.* Birmingham: University of Birmingham.

Lewis, J. and Glennerster, H. (1996) *Implementing the new community care.* Buckingham: Open University Press.

Lipsky, M. (1980) *Street level bureaucracy: dilemmas of the individual in public services.* New York: Russell Sage Foundation.

Lloyd, M., (2002) Care management. In R. Adams, L. Dominelli and M. Payne (eds), *Critical practice in social work.* Basingstoke: Palgrave Macmillan, pp159–68.

Local Government Ombudsman (2009) S*ix lives: the provision of public services to people with learning disabilities.* London: TSO.

Lyon, J. (2005) A systems approach to direct payments: a response to friend or foe? Towards a critical assessment of direct payments. *Critical Social Policy,* 25(2): 240–52.

Mandelstam, M. (2009) *Safeguarding vulnerable adults and the law.* London: Jessica Kingsley.

Mansell, J. (1994) Challenging behaviour: the prospect for change. *British Journal of Learning Disabilities,* 22: 2–5.

Mansell, J. and Beadle–Brown, J. (2003) Person-centred planning or person-centred action? *Journal of Applied Research in Intellectual Disabilities*, 17: 1–9.

Mansell, J. and Beadle-Brown J. (2004) Person-centred planning or person-centred action? A response to the commentaries. *Journal of Applied Research in Intellectual Disabilities*, 17: 31–5.

Mansell, J., Beadle-Brown, J., Cambridge, P., Milne, A. and Whelton, B. (2009) Adult protection incidence of referrals, nature and risk factors in two English local authorities. *Journal of Social Work*, 9(1): 23–38.

Mantell, A. (2008) Human rights and wrongs: The Human Rights Act 1998. In A. Mantell and T. Scragg (eds) *Safeguarding adults in social* work. London: Sage.

Manthorpe, J., Jacobs, S., Rapaport, J., Challis, D., Netten, A., Glendinning. C., Stevens, M., Wilberforce, M., Knapp, M. and Harris, J. (2008) Training for change: early days of individual budgets and the implications for social work and care management practice: a qualitative study of the views of trainers. *British Journal of Social Work*. Advance Access, 10.1093/bjsw/bcn017. Online: **http://php.york.ac.uk/inst/spru/pubs/617/** (accessed 2 July 2009).

Marshall, M. (1990) *Social work with old people.* London: Macmillan.

McDonald, A. (2001) Care in the community. In L.A. Cull and J. Roche (eds) *The law and social work.* London: The Open University, pp146–54.

McDonald, A., Postle, K. and Dawson, C. (2008) Barriers to retaining and using professional knowledge in local authority social work practice with adults in the UK. *British Journal of Social Work*, 38(7): 1370–87.

McGlaughlin, A., Gorfin, L. and Saul, C. (2004) Enabling adults with learning disabilities to articulate their housing needs. *British Journal of Social Work,* 34: 709–26.

Mead, G.H. (1934) *Mind, self and society.* Chicago: The University of Chicago Press.

Meagher, G. and Parton, N. (2004) Modernising social work and the ethics of care. *Social Work and Society*, 2(1): 10–27.

Means, R., Richards, S. and Smith, R. (2003) Community care policy and practice. 4th edn. Basingstoke: Palgrave Macmillan.

Mental Capacity Act 2005. (c.9). London: HMSO. Online: **www.opsi.gov.uk/acts/acts2005/ukpga_20050009_en_1** (accessed 1 July 2009).

Milner, J. and O'Byrne, P. (2002) *Assessment in social work.* 2nd edn. Basingstoke: Palgrave Macmillan.

Minichiello, V., Browne, J. and Kendig, H. (2000) Perceptions and consequences of ageism: views of older people. *Ageing and Society*, 20: 253–78.

Monk, J. (2006) Do direct payments offer people with learning disabilities greater choice and control? In K. Brown (ed), *Vulnerable adults and community care.* Exeter: Learning Matters Ltd.

Morris, J. (1993) *Independent lives.* Basingstoke: Macmillan Press.

Munro, E. (2004) The impact of audit on social work practice. *British Journal of Social Work*, 34: 1075–95.

National School of Government (2007) *Summary of public service reform.* London: Crown Copyright.

National Statistics. (2008) *Community care statistics 2006–2007: referrals, assessments and packages of care for adults in England.* London: The Information Centre.

Naylor, L. (2006) Adult protection for community care/vulnerable adults. In K. Brown (ed) *Vulnerable adults and community care.* Exeter: Learning Matters, pp111–27.

Nelson, G. and Prilleltensky, I. (eds) (2005) *Community psychology in pursuit of liberation and well-being.* Basingstoke: Palgrave Macmillan.

Nelson, T.D. (2005) Ageism: prejudice against our feared future self. *Journal of Social Issues,* 61(2): 207–21.

Newman, J. (2007) The 'double dynamics' of activation. *International Journal of Sociology and Social Policy,* 27(9/10): 364–75.

O'Keeffe, M., Hills, A., Doyle, M., Mc Cready, C., Scholes, S., Constantine, R., Tinker, A., Manthorpe, J., Biggs, S. and Erens, B. (2007) *UK study of the abuse and neglect of older people: prevalence survey report.* Kent: National Centre for Social Research.

Orme, J. (2002) Social work: gender, care and justice. *British Journal of Social Work,* 32: 799–814.

O'Sullivan, T. (2002) Managing risk and decision making. In R. Adams, L. Dominelli and M. Payne (eds), *Critical practice in social work.* Basingstoke: Palgrave Macmillan, pp269–76.

Parker, M. (1997) Organisations and citizenship. *Organisation,* 4(1): 75–92.

Parrott, L. (2006) *Values and ethics in social work practice.* Exeter: Learning Matters.

Percy-Smith, J. (1996) *Needs assessment in public policy.* Buckingham: Open University Press.

Pierson, J. and Thomas, M. (2002) *Dictionary of Social Work.* 2nd edn. Glasgow: HarperCollins.

Poll, C., Duffy, S., Hatton, C., Sanderson, H. and Routledge, M. (2006) *A report on In Control's first phase 2003–2005.* London: In Control.

Pratt, A. (2006) Neo-liberalism and social policy. In M. Lavalette and A. Pratt (eds), *Social policy theories, concepts and issues.* London: Sage.

Price, D. (2006) The poverty of older people in the UK. *Journal of Social Work Practice,* 20: 251–66.

Priestly, M. (1999) *Disability politics and community care.* London: Jessica Kingsley.

Prime Minister's Strategy Unit (2005) *Improving the life chances of disabled people.* London: The Strategy Unit.

Pritchard, J. (2001) Introduction. In J. Pritchard (ed) *Good practice with vulnerable adults.* Philadelphia: Jessica Kingsley.

Ramon, S. (2008) Neoliberalism and its implications for mental health in the UK. *International Journal of Law and Psychiatry,* 31: 116–25.

Rapley, M. (2004) *Social construction of intellectual disability.* New York: Cambridge University Press.

Ray, M. and Phillips, J. (2002) Older people. In R. Adams, L. Dominelli and M. Payne (eds), *Critical practice in social work.* Basingstoke: Palgrave Macmillan.

Richards, S. (2000) Bridging the divide: elders and the assessment process. *British Journal of Social Work*, 30: 37–49.

Riddell, S., Pearson, M., Jolly, D., Barnes, C., Priestly, M. and Mercer, G. (2005) The development of direct payments in the UK: implications for social justice. *Social Policy and Society*, 4(1): 75–85.

Riddell, S., Priestley, M., Pearson, C., Mercer, G., Barnes, C., Jolly, D. and Williams, V. (2006) *Disabled people and direct payments: a UK comparative study*. Swindon: ESRC. Online: **www.leeds.ac.uk/ disability-studies/projects/UKdirectpayments/UKDPfinal.pdf** (accessed 2 July 2009).

Rogowski, S. (2009) A twin track to trouble. *Professional Social Work: BASW*, June: 26–7.

Samuel, M. (2007) Direct payments and individual budgets. *Community Care*, 22 February.

Sanderson, H. (2000) *Person centred planning: key features and approaches*. York: Joseph Rowntree Foundation.

Scourfield, P. (2005) Implementing the Community Care (Direct Payments) Act: Will the supply of personal assistants meet the demand and at what price? *Journal of Social Policy*, 34(3): 469–88.

Scourfield, P. (2007) Social care and the modern citizen: client, consumer, service user, manager and entrepreneur. *British Journal of Social Work*, 37(1): 107–22.

Secker, J., Hill, R., Villeneau, L. and Parkman, S. (2003) Promoting independence: but promoting what and how? *Ageing and Society*, 23: 375–391.

Sellars, C.W. (2002) *Risk assessment in people with learning disabilities*. Oxford: Blackwell Publishing.

Sevenhuijsen, S. (2000) Caring in the third way: the relation between obligation, responsibility and care in third way discourse. *Critical Social Policy*, 20(5): 5–37.

Sharkey, P. (2000) *The essentials of community care*. Basingstoke: Palgrave Macmillan.

Simpson, M. (2002) Bodies, brains, behaviour: the return of the three stooges in learning disability. In M. Corker and S. French (eds), *Disability discourse*. Buckingham: Open University Press.

Skidmore, D. (1994) *The ideology of community care*. London: Chapman and Hall.

Smale, G., Tuson, G. and Statham, D. (2000) *Social work and social problems: working towards inclusion and social change*. Basingstoke: Palgrave Macmillan.

Smith, K. (2005) *Response prepared by the British Institute of Learning Disabilities to the green paper independence, well-being and choice*. Kidderminster: BILD.

Social Care Institute of Excellence (2005) *SCIE research briefing 11: the health and well-being of young carers*. London: SCIE.

Social Care Institute of Excellence (2008) *Personalisation: a rough guide*. London: SCIE.

Spandler, H. (2004) Friend or foe? Towards a critical assessment of direct payments. *Critical Social Policy*, 24(2): 187–209.

Stainton, T. (2002) Learning disability. In R. Adams, L. Dominelli and M. Payne (eds), *Critical practice in social work*. Basingstoke: Palgrave Macmillan, pp190–8.

Stanley, N., Manthorpe, J. and White, M. (2007) Depression in the profession: social workers' experiences and perceptions. *British Journal of Social Work*, 37(2): 281–98.

Stapleton, S. (2008) Can you feel the buzz of care management transformation? *Community Care*, 12 June: 29.

Stevens, A. (2004) Closer to home: a critique of British government policy towards accommodating learning disabled people in their own home. *Critical Social Policy*, 24(2): 233–54.

Stuart-Hamilton, I. (2000) *The psychology of ageing: an introduction.* London: Jessica Kingsley.

Swain, J., French, S. and Cameron, C. (2003) *Controversial issues in a disabling society.* Buckingham: Open University Press.

Tanner, D. (1997) Empowerment and care management: swimming against the tide. *Health and Social Care in the Community*, 6(6): 447–57.

Tanner, D. and Harris, J. (2008) *Working with older people.* Abingdon: Routledge.

Taylor-Gooby, P. and Lawson, R. (1993) *Markets and managers: new issues in the delivery of welfare.* Buckinghamshire: Open University Press.

Thomas, D. and Woods, H. (2003) *Working with people with learning disabilities.* London: Jessica Kingsley.

Thompson, N. (1998) *Promoting equality: challenging discrimination and oppression in the human services.* London: Macmillan.

Thompson, N. (2001) *Anti-discriminatory practice.* 3rd edn. Basingstoke: Palgrave Macmillan.

Thompson, N. (2002) Social work with adults. In R. Adams, L. Dominelli and M. Payne (eds), *Social work: themes, issues and critical debates.* 2nd edn. Basingstoke: Palgrave Macmillan, pp287–307.

Thompson, N. (2003) *Promoting equality: challenging discrimination and oppression.* Basingstoke: Palgrave Macmillan.

Thompson, N. (2006) *Anti-discriminatory practice.* 4th edn. Basingstoke: Palgrave Macmillan.

Tindall, B. (1997) People with learning difficulties: citizenship, personal development and the management of risk. In H. Kemshall and J. Pritchard (eds), *Good practice in risk assessment and risk management 2.* London: Jessica Kingsley, pp103–17.

Titterton, M. (1999) Training professionals in risk assessment and risk management. What does the research tell us? In P. Parsloe (ed), *Risk assessment in social care and social work.* London: Jessica Kingsley.

Titterton, M. (2005) *Risk and risk taking in health and social welfare.* London: Jessica Kingsley.

Tronto, J.C. (1993) *Moral boundaries: a political argument for an ethic of care.* New York: Routledge.

Tsui, M. and Cheung. F.C.H. (2004) Gone with the wind: the impacts of managerialism on human services. *British Journal of Social Work*, 34: 437–42.

Twigg, J. and Atkin, K. (2002) *Carers' perceived policy and practice in informal care.* Maidenhead: Oxford University Press.

Vincent, J.A. (1999) *Politics, power and old age.* Buckingham: Open University Press.

Waine, B. (2000) Managing performance through pay. In J. Clarke, S. Gewirtz and E. McLaughlin (eds), *New managerialism, new welfare*. London: Sage.

Walker, A. and Walker, C. (1998) Normalisation and 'normal' ageing: the social construction of dependency among older people with learning difficulties. *Disability and Society*, 13(1): 125–42.

Waller, B.N. (2005) *Consider ethics: theory, reading and contemporary issues*. New York: Pearson Longman.

Waterson, J. (1998) Redefining community care social work: needs or risk led? *Health and Social Care in the Community*, 7(4): 276–9.

Williams, P. (2006) *Social work with people with learning difficulties*. Exeter: Learning Matters.

Woods, N. (2006) International political economy in an age of globalisation. In J. Baylis and S. Smith (eds), *The globalisation of world politics*. Oxford: Oxford University Press.

Index

Abercrombie, N. et al. 95
abuse: of older people 11, 13, 27–8; by
    unregulated assistants 78, 79
Adams, R. 84
adult protection 11, 27–8
Age Concern 38
ageing process 17–18; life-course approach 31
ageism 17, 21, 25, 26
Ahmed, W.I.U. 86
Alcock, P. et al. 84
anti-oppressive practice 81–4; core assumptions
    82; definition 82; with learning disabilities
    57; with older people 31; principles 82–3
Askheim, O.P. 78
assessment models 55–6
assistance as care 67–8
Atkin, K. 35, 38, 39, 46, 47

Bain, A. 24
Barber, P. 29
Barnett, M. 10
Bates, P. 66
Bauld, L. et al. 78
Beadle-Brown, J. 6, 59–60
Beckett, C. 75
Benjamin, A. 43
Beresford, P. 6, 37, 38
Better Services for the Mentally Handicapped
    52
Beveridge Report (1942) 37
Biggs, S. et al. 21
(BIHR) British Institute of Human Rights (2008)
    13
Billig, M. 36
binary opposites 95–6
Black and Minority Ethnic people 80–1
Blair, T. 39
Bornat, J. 86
Bowers, H. et al. 10
Braye, S. 57, 58, 62
Brechin, A. et al. 86
British Institute of Human Rights (BIHR) (2008)
    13
Brown, G. 45
Brown, K. 37
Brown, L. 78
Brown, R. 29
Buller, J. 98

Burnham, P. 98–9
Burns, J.M. 100

Cambridge, P. 54, 56, 57, 58, 59, 60
Cameron, C. 94
capacity 57
care 33–48; as a commodity 10, 37; definition
    35; feminism and ethics of care 36–7, 38;
    legislation 38, 39, 40; and personalisation
    40–1; political context 37–40; The Pro–Am
    Revolution 40–1; professional social work
    40–2; reasons for caring 35–6; see also
    informal carers
care by the community 53
care in the community 53
care management 57–9, 60, 93; resource
    allocation 58–9; support coordination
    57–8, 60
Carers (Equal Opportunities) Act (2004) 40
Carers (Recognition and Services) Act (1995) 39
Carers and Disabled Children Act 2000 39, 46,
    47, 72
Carers at the Heart of 21st Century Families and
    Communities 43
Carer's Strategy (Caring about Carers) 39, 43
Carers UK 38, 44–5
Carey, M. 6, 10, 96, 99
Caring for People 39, 53
Carmichael, A. 78
Carnaby, S. 54, 57, 58, 59, 60
Carr, S. 4, 7
Carson, D. 24
Cartwright, R. 42
Cemlyn, S. 105
Cheung, F.C.H. 101
choice 4, 10–12, 19, 66, 87, 96–8
Clark, H. et al. 71, 80, 86
Clarke, J. 10, 96–7
Clegg, S. 97
Clements, J. 62, 63, 65
Clements, L. 40, 44, 47, 51–2, 72
Code of Ethics for Social Workers 76, 105
coercion 97–8
Collins, S. 98
Commission for Social Care Inspection (CSCI) 4,
    13, 40, 44, 77, 85, 97
community care 51–3, 55; see also NHS and
    Community Care Act 1990

Community Care (Direct Payments) Act (1996) 72

comparative need 54

consumerist approach 10–12

Cope, S. 99

Courpasson, D. 97

critical need 54

Croft, S. 6

CSCI see Commission for Social Care Inspection

cultural beliefs 7, 25, 62, 63–4

culturally relevant services 80–1

Dany, F. 97

Davey et al. 77–8

Davies, M. 71–2

Davis, F. 66

decisional autonomy 19

dementia 19, 27

dependence: cultural construction of 7, 66; older people 18–19

depoliticisation and social care 98–9

Deprivation of Liberty Safeguards (DOLS) 30, 102

dichotomous thinking 95

direct payments 70–87; anti-oppressive practice 81–4; barriers to take-up 77; Black and Minority Ethnic people 80–1; definition 4; developing good practice 80–1; direct payments in practice 44, 76–8; eligibility 11, 23–4, 42, 72–3, 77; implications for future 84–6; interdependency 20; learning disabilities 70; older people 7, 23–4, 70, 71, 72, 76, 78, 80, 94, 97; and personalisation 74; professional discretion and values 75–6; and risk 78–80; role of social worker 74, 76–7; socio-political context 71–3

disability, individuals with 3

Disabled People and Direct Payments 73

Disabled Persons (Services, Consultation and Representation) Act (1986) 71

discourse 95

discrimination: definitions 9, 84; and oppression 9, 31, 63–4, 67, 99

discriminatory abuse 28

disengagement theory 17–18

diversity 53

DOLS see Deprivation of Liberty Safeguards

domestic violence 28

Dominelli, L. 67, 82

economic rationality 10

EHRC see Equality and Human Rights Commission

eligibility for services 40; carers 43–4; direct payments 11, 23–4, 42, 72–3, 77; discretion 75; funding panels 97; learning disabilities 54, 58, 67, 68; older people 19, 23–4; self-funders 8–9, 23–4

eligible need 54

Ellis, K. 75

Emerson, E. 67

emotional abuse 28

Eppard, R.G. 100

Equality and Human Rights Commission (EHRC) 102, 103–4

ethics of care 36–7, 38, 76, 105

European Convention on Human Rights 13

exchange model of assessment 55–6, 57

expressed need 56

Fair Access to Care Services (FACs) 8–9, 23, 44, 54, 58, 68

felt need 56

feminism and ethics of care 36–7, 38

Ferguson, I. 92, 94, 96, 97

financial abuse 28

Fisher, B. 35

Flinders, M. 98

Fook, J. 66, 95

Foster, M. et al. 4

Foucault, M. 95

'fourth age' 21

funding panels 97

Galpin, D. 55, 100

Gilbert, P. 50

Glasby, J. 71

Glendinning, C. et al. 4, 6, 8, 85

Glennerster, H. 52

globalisation 38

Goodship, J. 99

Gorman, H. 78, 104

Griffith's report (1988) 53

Gross, R. 17

Hagestad, G. O. 19

Hall, P.M. 97

Harris, J. 74, 77, 80, 85

Hasler, F. et al. 79, 86

Hatton, C. et al. (2008) 4

Health and Social Care Act (2001) 72

Health and Social Care Act (2008) 13, 42, 72

Healy, K. 82–3

Healy, L.M. 14, 102

Henwood, M. 3, 44, 89

Horner, L. 93

Hudson, B. 3, 8–9, 42, 44

human rights 65; and personalisation 12–15, 87
Human Rights Act (1998) 102, 103–4, 105; articles 12; and learning disabilities 26–7; and older people 29; and personalisation 13
human rights-based approach: to MPT 101–4; in practice 104–5
Humphreys, B. 99
Huxley, P. et al. 93, 94

IBs *see* individual budgets
ideology 36, 37
Ife, J. 14, 65, 96, 102–3, 105
ILF (Independent Living Fund) 71
IMCA (Independent Mental Capacity Advocate) 29
'Improving the life chances of disabled people' 3
In Control 7
independence: cultural construction of 66; and learning disabilities 64–8; of older people 19–20
Independence, Well-being and Choice 42, 85, 91
The Independent Living 1993 Fund 71
Independent Living Fund (ILF) 71
Independent Mental Capacity Advocate (IMCA) 29
individual budgets (IBs) 1, 6–8, 42, 44; choice 98; definition 4, 51, 74; older people 7, 75, 85, 94
informal carers 33–4; attitudes to own role 47; changing role 42–5; as co-service users 46, 47; as co-workers 46, 47; legislation 38, 39, 40; models of 45–7; needs 20, 44, 47; and personalisation 40–1; poverty 44–5; reasons for caring 35–6; as resources 45, 46; superseded carers 46; support for 44–5, 46; turnover 44
institutional abuse 28
intelligence quotient (IQ) 50
interdependence 20, 36, 67
International Federation of Social Workers 105

Johns, R. 29
Jones, A. 93
Jones, C. 42, 93
Jordan, B. 10, 38, 39, 41
Joseph Rowntree Foundation 81

Kemshall, H. 26

labelling 61–2, 67, 68
language 83; and ambiguity 95–8, 99; and power relations 22, 95, 96
Lawson, R. 99

Le Grand, J. et al. 10, 11, 12, 13
Le Mesurier, N. et al. 6
Leadbeater, C. et al. 2, 4, 5–6, 10, 40–1, 91, 94, 98, 99
leadership 99–100
learning disabilities 49–69; assessment models 55–6; capacity 57; care management 57–9; caring role of 67; cognitive functioning 50; communication skills 50, 65; community care 51–3, 55; definition 50–1; direct payments 70; eligibility for services 54, 58, 67, 68; empowerment 55, 57, 58, 60, 65, 67, 68; human rights 26–7; independence 64–8; labelling 61–2, 67, 68; needs assessment 53–4, 56, 58; normalisation 53; older people with 19; person-centred planning 4, 59–60, 64–8; personalisation 51–3, 57–9; rights-based approach 54–5; risk 56–7, 62–3, 68; social functioning 50; social inclusion 59, 61–4, 66–7; vulnerability 64–8
Leece, J. 10, 79, 86
legislation 26–30, 38, 39, 40
Lewis, I. 43
Lewis, J. 52
life cycle model 31
Lipsky, M. 75
Littlechild, R. 71
Lloyd, M. 57
local authorities 6, 39, 40, 41, 42, 54, 55, 57; direct payments 71, 72, 73, 79, 81, 84, 97
Local Government Ombudsman 102
Lyon, J. 84

McDonald, A. 53
McGlaughlin, A. et al. 65
managerialism 101
Mandelstam, M. 11–12, 51, 57, 72–3
Mansell, J. et al. 6, 11, 59–60, 62
Mantell, A. 13
Manthorpe, J. et al. 94
marginalisation 5–9
Martin, N. 62, 63, 65
Maynard, A. 75
Mead, G.H. 83
Meagher, G. 36, 37, 38
Means, R. et al. 53, 55
medical discourse 22
Mental Capacity Act (2005) 26–7, 29, 57, 65, 102
Miller, P. 40–1
Milner, J. 55, 67
modernisation 1, 2–3, 41, 88, 89–90; human rights-based approach 101–4; key principles 90

Modernising Social Services 2–3, 41, 89
Monk, J. 72
Morris, J. 66, 67
MPT (modernisation, personalisation and transformation) *see* modernisation; personalisation; public sector reform; transformation
Munro, E. 97–8

National Improvement and Efficiency Strategy 100
National Indicator Set 98
National Service Framework (NSF) for Older People 27
Naylor, L. 62
needs: carers 20, 44, 47; learning disabilities 53–4, 56, 58; vs rights 102, 103
neglect: and the law 28; of older people 11, 27–8
Nelson, G. and Prilleltensky, I. (2005) 5
neo-liberalism 38–9
Newman, J. 14
NHS and Community Care Act 1990 39, 51, 52, 53, 58, 72
Nicholas, S. 45
No Secrets 28, 50–1
normative need 54
NSF (National Service Framework for Older People) 27

O'Byrne, P. 55, 67
O'Keeffe, M. et al. 11
older people 16–32; abuse 11, 13, 27–8; ageing process 17–18, 31; anti-oppressive practice 31; dependence and independence 18–20; eligibility for services 19, 23–4; empowerment 22, 29; human rights 29; individual budgets 7, 75, 85, 94; with learning difficulties 19; legislation 26–30; life-course approach 31; neglect 11, 27–8; population 41, 85; power and oppression 20–2; resources and inequality 23–4; support services 80; working with risk 24–6; *see also* direct payments
oppression: in assessment 55; definition 9; and discrimination 9, 31, 63–4, 67, 99; *see also* anti-oppressive practice
O'Sullivan, T. 62–3
Our Health, Our Care, Our Say 5, 42, 44, 85, 90, 91

Parker, J.L. 100
Parker, M. 97
participative approach 4

partnership working 83, 86
Parton, N. 36, 37, 38
PAs *see* personal assistants
person-centred planning (PCP) 1, 4, 6, 7, 59–60, 64–8, 73
Person-Centred Risk Assessment and Management Plan 24
personal assistants (PAs) 78–9, 80
personal budgets 1, 4, 5–6, 7, 74
personalisation 1–2, 88; and care management 57–9; carers 40–1; choice 4, 10–12, 19, 66, 96–8; and community care 51–3; consumerist approach 10–12; definitions 3, 73–4, 96; and direct payments 74; and discrimination 9–10, 99; and eligibility 44; and human rights 12–15, 87; human rights-based approach 101–4; impact on practitioners 94; impact on users 94, 97, 99; and marginalisation 5–9; and oppression 9–10, 99; paradox of personalisation 6, 99; and social care reform 3–5, 90–2, 99
physical abuse 28
Pierson, J. 61
Postle, K. 104
poverty 21, 23, 38, 44–5
power: empowerment 22, 29, 55, 57, 58, 60, 65, 67, 68, 78, 83; labelling 61–2, 67, 68; and language 22, 95, 96; learning disabilities 55, 57, 58, 60, 61, 65, 67, 68; older people 20–2, 29
Preston-Shoot, M. 57, 58, 62
Priestly, M. 54, 72
Princess Royal Trust for Carers 45
Pritchard, J. 68
The Pro–Am Revolution 40–1
procedural model of assessment 55
professional discretion 75–6
public sector reform 1–3, 88–106; depoliticisation and social care 98–9; human rights-based approach 101–4; impact on practitioners 93–5; language and ambiguity 95–8, 99; leadership and management 99–101; modernisation 89–90; personalisation 3–5, 90–2, 99; transformation 92–3, 99–100
Putting People First 5, 41, 51–2, 85, 91

Rapley, M. 51, 61
Redmond, I. 44–5
residential care 19, 63–4, 97
resource allocation model 58–9
resource allocation system (RAS) 51

resources: choice 97; financial resources of older people 23–4; informal carers as 45, 46; services for older people 23–4
Riddell, S. et al. 77
rights and responsibilities 39, 45
rights-based approach 54–5, 102–3
risk: assessment 24, 56–7; and direct payments 78–80; and learning disabilities 56–7, 62–3, 68; and older people 24–6; stereotypes 25
Robbins, D. 4, 7
Rogowski, S. 96
rules 97–8, 100

Safeguarding Adults 27–8
Samuel, M. 70
Sanderson, H. 59, 67
Scope 84
Scourfield, P. 6, 13, 78–9
Secker, J. et al. 7, 20
self-determination 66, 68
self-esteem 25, 40
self-funding 8–9, 23–4
Sellars, C.W. 56, 57
Sevenhuijensen, S. 37
sexual abuse 28
Sharkey, P. 45–6
Simpson, M. 67
Skidmore, D. 72, 85
Smale, G. et al. 55
Smith, K. 68
social inclusion 40, 59, 61–4, 66–7
social justice 37
social networks 62
social workers: changing role 41–2, 74, 76–7; impact of reform 93–5
Spandler, H. 79, 85
Stainton, T. 66, 67
Stancliffe, R. 67
Stanley, N. et al. 93
stereotypes 25, 62, 63

Stuart-Hamilton, I. 31
support coordination 57–8, 60
Swain, J. et al. 62

Tanner, D. 54, 56, 59, 77, 80, 85
Taylor-Gooby, P. 99
'third age' 21
third sector role 41–2
Third Way 39–40, 45, 84–5
Thomas, D. 53, 67
Thomas, M. 61
Thompson, N. 9, 17, 22, 25, 31, 36, 63, 65, 66, 82, 84, 95
Tindal, B. 63, 65
transactional leadership 100
transformation 2, 88, 92–3, 95; human rights-based approach 101–4; leadership and management 99–101
transformational leadership 100, 103
Transforming Social Care LAC 92–3
Tronto, J. 35
Tronto, J.C. 35, 37
Tsui, M. 101
Twigg, J. 35, 38, 39, 46, 47

Uhlenberg, P. 19

values 9–10, 25, 62, 75–6
Valuing People 50, 59, 64, 67
Valuing People Now 59
Vincent, J.A. 21

Walker, A. 19
Walker, C. 19
Waterson, J. 56, 57, 60
welfare capitalism 37, 38
Williams, P. 50
Woods, H. 53, 67
Woods, N. 10

young carers 43